THE
MONEY
SPINNER
Monte Carlo Casino

By the same author

THE
MONEY
SPINNER

Monte Carlo Casino

XAN FIELDING

Weidenfeld and Nicolson
London

Weidenfeld and Nicolson
11 St John's Hill   London SW11

ISBN 0 297 77201 5

Printed and bound in Great Britain by
Morrison & Gibb Ltd, London and Edinburgh

For Magouche

The roulette wheel has no memory and no conscience.

DOSTOEVSKY

CONTENTS

ILLUSTRATIONS

ACKNOWLEDGMENTS

The authorities of whom I have availed myself are listed in *Bibliography and References*, pp. 193–9. My thanks are due to the authors I have mentioned, and to their respective publishers, for allowing me to cull and quote from copyright material.

I also owe a special debt to Patrick Leigh Fermor, who applied himself to my typescript and 'raked it', as he put it, 'with the eye of a friendly hawk'. What merit the final version has is due in large part to his criticism and advice.

X. F.

1

THE BANKRUPT PRINCIPALITY

On 1 March 1815, towards eleven o'clock at night, a berlin travelling eastwards along the coast road of the South of France was stopped by a troop of armed soldiers just outside the little village of Cannes. Its solitary occupant – a man of consequence, judging by his escort and outriders – was summoned to step down from the carriage and establish his identity. This he haughtily refused to do until, to his amazement, he recognized the officer in charge of the troop: General Cambronne, one of Napoleon's staunchest supporters, who had followed the defeated emperor to Elba.

Having announced his name and title – Prince Honoré-Gabriel Grimaldi – the traveller was at once informed of the reason for his arrest: Napoleon had just escaped from his island prison and, wishing to avoid the garrison at Antibes on whose loyalty he dared not count, had landed on this deserted stretch of coast that very afternoon. For security reasons, orders had been given to intercept and detain anyone who happened to be in the vicinity. Prince Honoré-Gabriel was therefore required to interrupt his journey for a few hours. In the meantime he was conducted to a nearby olive grove where, beside a camp fire, he found himself face to face with the man whom all Europe believed to be still in exile.

The interview was cordial, for the prince was no stranger to the imperial family. Napoleon was in high spirits and gaily inquired where the traveller was going.

'Home,' the prince replied. 'To Monaco.'

'I too am going home,' said the emperor. 'To the Tuileries.'

In the early hours of the morning the imperial troops moved off in the direction of Grasse, and Napoleon, having wished the prince good luck, continued on his road.

Prince Honoré-Gabriel could hardly have foreseen the rapidity of the emperor's downfall, but he was aware of the political upheavals that were bound to ensue from his reappearance. He therefore hastened to send a report of the fortuitous meeting to the Minister of War, Marshal Soult – 'with a handful of soldiers at Cannes,' he declared, 'it would have been easy to prevent Napoleon from landing' – and on his way through Antibes he requested the general in command of the garrison for the immediate dispatch of a French contingent to Monaco.

This request was by no means unusual. During several centuries the princes of Monaco, to maintain the independence of their state, had of their own free will invited the protection of Spain and France alternately. Thanks to this protection the Grimaldis were now the oldest sovereign family in Europe and up to the time of the French Revolution had possessed, in addition to the three communes of Menton, Roquebrune and Monaco which comprised the principality, the dukedom of Valentinois, the marquisate of Les Baux, the countship of Carladès and numerous other fiefs. During the night of 4 August 1789, however, the National Constituent Assembly abolished all the feudal rights and privileges enjoyed by the aristocracy, and the princes were thus deprived of the income they derived from their large and valuable estates. Six months later, on 20 January 1790, the principality was declared a republic and the revolutionary councillors of the three communes decreed the perpetual dethronement of the House of Grimaldi.

Honoré-Gabriel was eleven years of age at the time, old enough to appreciate the extent of the disaster. Worse was to follow. On 25 September 1783, at the height of the Terror, all the members of his family in France were arrested under the 'Law of Suspects'. His old grandfather, formerly the reigning prince, Honoré III, who had come to Paris in the hope of saving the family fortune, was imprisoned in the barracks of the Rue de Sèvres. His epileptic father, the Duc de Valentinois, who had never even left the country, was nevertheless counted as an *émigré* and likewise imprisoned. His mother, denounced as 'a demon of licentiousness and debauchery', had been divorced by her husband a few months previously; but she too, with his younger brother Florestan, was arrested and held prisoner in the Couvent des Anglaises.

His uncle Joseph and his twenty-six-year-old aunt Françoise-Thérèse de Choiseul-Stainville, having entrusted their children to a reliable guardian, had taken refuge abroad in the early days of the Revolution. But this long absence proved unendurable for the young mother and she returned to France to see her two daughters. Arrested as a 'suspect', she was promptly condemned to death for being 'a declared enemy of the people, for having relations while abroad with the enemies of the Republic, for supplying them with help and preparing, in complicity with tyrants and by all sorts of criminal manoeuvres, the destruction of national representation and the restoration of tyranny.'

On the advice of a friend she announced that she was with child and her execution was therefore postponed; but on second thoughts, disdaining such a subterfuge, she addressed a letter to Fouquier-Tinville, the Public Prosecutor of the Revolutionary Tribunal, asking him to come and see her. Then, with a piece of broken glass, she cut off her hair as a keepsake for her children. There was no reply from Fouquier-Tinville, so she wrote to him again:

> I must inform you, citizen, that I am not pregnant . . . I did not befoul my mouth with this lie from fear of death or to avoid it, but only in order to cut off my hair myself. It is the only legacy I can leave my children, and this at least must not be sullied by the hands of the executioner.

Her letter was signed 'CHOISEUL-STAINVILLE, JOSEPH GRIMALDI-MONACO, a foreign princess dying through the injustice of French judges'.

On the same day the order for her execution reached the prison.

The rest of the Grimaldis were saved from the guillotine only twenty-four hours later by the 9 Thermidor, when the Terror came to an end and most of the 'suspects' were released; but the old prince, as the father of an *émigré*, was still kept prisoner. He was not set free till 5 October 1794; and six months later, broken with age, infirmities and the hardships of his long incarceration, he died in his house in the Rue de Varennes and was succeeded by his eldest son, Honoré-Gabriel's father, now known as Monsieur de Valentinois. The Grimaldis now found themselves reduced to the greatest straits. Under the Consulate and the Empire they might have obtained good posts, for the new régime was anxious to attract the recently dispossessed nobility; but Valentinois's illness compelled him to live in semi-retirement in the country, while his brother Joseph, who had by now returned from England, was forced by penury to seek service in Napoleon's army.

Honoré-Gabriel, who was twenty, followed his uncle's example. He enlisted in the 23rd Hussars and was commissioned a year later. He served under General Grouchy in the Army of the Rhine and in 1800 was promoted to the rank of lieutenant on the field of Hohenlinden, where he was also seriously wounded by a bullet in the arm. He had become Grouchy's aide-de-camp by now and he appeared to be heading for a brilliant military career, like his grandfather and most of his ancestors. His wound, however, combined with his failing health, forced him to retire from the army for a few years. But in 1806 he rejoined his general and covered himself with fresh glory. At the battle of Prenzlau, with a handful of cavalry, he forced an entire Prussian battalion to surrender. Again, during the Silesian campaign of 1808, he charged a strongly held infantry position and brought back three hundred prisoners, though wounded in the arm this time by the enemy's bayonets.

This exploit earned him the Legion of Honour and a captaincy, but his wounds made him unfit for active service and on 7 June 1809 he became an equerry to the Empress Josephine, to whom his uncle was already a chamberlain. In the following year he was created a Baron of the Empire. He figured in the *Almanach Impérial* as 'Baron de Monaco', though he still insisted on his subordinates addressing him by his former title. This insistence was in keeping with an inherited taste for splendour: his grandfather had been famous for his love of luxury and display. A smart turnout had become a mania with him – the shortest carriage journeys involved six horses, outriders and a running footman.

The Grimaldis thus enjoyed some position. No doubt they shared in the golden shower that fell on all the nobles who rallied to the new régime, but it was no compensation for their lost estates. The victory of the Allies, the fall of the Empire and the restoration of the monarchy brought the hope that Monaco might recover its independence: in 1793, when Nice was reunited to France, the principality had been absorbed into the newly created department of the Alpes Maritimes. This hope was fulfilled. On the margin of the project for the remodelling of the map of Europe – the draft was ultimately confirmed at the treaty of Paris – Talleyrand wrote: 'The Prince of Monaco will be restored'; and the treaty stipulated that France renounced all claim to the county of Nice. 'The principality of Monaco, however,' it went on, 'is replaced in the position in which it found itself before 1 January 1792.' Thus, though they lost their estates in France, the Grimaldis recovered their ancient patrimony. Honoré-Gabriel's father took the title of Prince Honoré iv.

But being too old and ill to reign, he appointed his brother Joseph in his stead. Predictably Honoré-Gabriel protested against this, and more so since his uncle lingering in Paris ruled through an acting governor. He himself, he claimed, as heir apparent, should be the one to administer the principality; and the claim was eventually recognized. Towards the end of February 1815 he left Paris on the first stage of his journey home.

During the twenty years when the principality was attached to France the inhabitants had enjoyed comparative peace and quiet. Only once – on 23 May 1800, when a raiding party from a British frigate blew up the local powder magazine and killed a number of women and children – had they been reminded of the realities of war. But the last years of Napoleon's reign had been hard. Their chronic poverty had been much aggravated during the winter of 1813–14, when the blockade had ruined their exports and an unusual spell of frost had all but wiped out the lemon and olive crops. The republican fervour of the early days of the Revolution had long since been succeeded by a deep regret for their prosperity as a French protectorate under the feudal Grimaldis. They welcomed Prince Honoré-Gabriel with an explosion of joy.

His own delight, however, was now accompanied by a feeling of foreboding which he had not been able to shed since his encounter with Napoleon. The emperor's reappearance was yet another threat to Monaco's newly restored independence. As soon as the prince was back in his palace, he renewed his earlier request for the dispatch of a French garrison.

The palace had suffered during the absence of its rightful occupants. It had been systematically pillaged during the Revolutionary years, and the furniture and the treasures which the long line of the Grimaldis had accumulated over the centuries were auctioned off and sold to the highest bidder. In 1802 the building had been converted into a hospital for the republican armies in Italy. In 1812 it was the local almshouse and by June 1814, when the last of its inmates had been evacuated, little remained but a gutted and evil-smelling shell. Restoration was urgent but, before Prince Honoré-Gabriel could begin, an even more pressing matter cropped up. During the afternoon of 13 March, only ten days after his arrival, a contingent of Anglo-Italian troops landed in the harbour. The British commanding officer, Colonel Burke, presented the prince with a letter from the governor of the County of Nice announcing the Allied decision to occupy Monaco. 'I feel sure,' the letter ended, 'that your Serene Highness will appreciate this necessity when he realizes the developments that are bound to take place in France as a result of Bonaparte's reappearance.'

The prince had realized them for some time, but he failed to see that anything could be gained by an occupation of the principality. In the circumstances, however, he could only acquiesce. As a sop to his subjects, whose memory of the 1800 raid had scarcely encouraged them to welcome British troops, he lodged a formal protest and asked the French ambassador at Turin to request an explanation from the Sardinian government. But before these negotiations could be completed, his worst fears were fulfilled. When the Hundred Days ended at Waterloo, Sardinia was quick to claim her share of the spoils, and the subsequent peace treaty abolished Monaco's connection with France and ordained that 'these relations will now exist between the principality and the King of Sardinia'. Honoré-Gabriel and his subjects thus found themselves, without even having been consulted in the matter, under the protection of an inveterate enemy.

The immediate consequences of the change were keenly felt. Gone was the free trade with France which had been so advantageous to the principality. Instead of this, all the conditions imposed by Sardinia tended to impoverish the Monégasques. The tobacco manufactory, Monaco's only industry and an important source of revenue, was forcibly suppressed. To make matters worse, the first summer under the new protectorate was marked by persistent rain and unusual cold which ruined the harvest. Gone too was the hope of compensation, estimated at four and a half million francs,* for the income which the Grimaldis had lost from the confiscation of their estates in France. Yet funds required for administering the principality had to be found. For this purpose Prince Honoré-Gabriel claimed a civil list of three hundred thousand francs – four times as much as his grandfather – and ruthless and immediate taxation was the only means of producing so large a sum.

Monaco was an essentially agricultural territory. In a matter of weeks a tax was imposed on every lemon and on every drop of exported oil. A fine was imposed for each head of cattle slaughtered without government sanction and for each tree cut down without a licence. Worse still, a monopoly for providing grain and making bread was granted to a Marseilles businessman by the name of Chapon, and his exploitation of the concession was damaging to the community. 'Behind the mask of a foreigner,' the prince thus became, in the words of a contemporary, 'the farmer, miller and baker of his country.'

At the same time, to silence the rumble of discontent, the old feudal system, abandoned at the time of the Revolution and no longer mitigated by the economic advantages which formerly accrued from the French protectorate, was now reintroduced. Prince Honoré-Gabriel ruled as a despot in his father's name, and

* The exchange rates at the time were 25 francs to the pound sterling, and 5 francs to the dollar.

after his father's death – the old prince was accidentally drowned in the Seine in April 1819 – he continued so to rule, as Honoré v, in his own. Though harshness was masked by fine manners, wit, tact and a noble presence, he behaved it was said, 'like an English landlord towards his Irish tenants'. It was an apt comparison.

He infinitely preferred the salons of Paris or his country house in Normandy, and his absences from the principality were protracted. Apart from four short periods – the five months immediately following his arrival, the winter of 1817–18, the first four months of 1822, and a final sojourn later that year – his entire reign was spent in France.

He was thus less aware than he might have been of his growing unpopularity. Yet many of the measures he introduced were specifically designed to assist the population. His policy was to supplement the slender revenues of the principality by the organization of state industries, but these industries proved incompatible with the Monégasque mentality and with the local economic situation. Among his other enterprises, he attempted to establish a lace factory, a perfumery and a workshop for straw-plaiting and hat-making, but his subjects disliked this sort of employment. They preferred to work in the open air, and in any case the Sardinian customs barrier prevented them from selling their produce abroad. He tried to abolish begging by grouping all the beggars in productive cooperatives, but the beggars preferred to beg. So he founded a poorhouse for them, but the cost of this philanthropic gesture could only be met by compulsory subscriptions, and this gave further grounds for complaint. He decided to exploit his right of striking his own money. But his silver pieces of five francs and his five-centime copper coins were so inferior that, over the border, the French refused to handle them.

Most of his reforms thus came to nothing, but he was not entirely to blame. Although his good intentions were often frustrated by his authoritarian methods, he was not so much an inefficient martinet as a victim of the times. Had he been born half a century later, he might have been regarded as a state socialist, or at any rate 'a gas-and-water, municipal-enterprise' socialist. His views might have won favour. His own opinion of himself was summed up in the words which he asked to be inscribed on his tomb: *'Ci gît qui voulu faire le bien* – Here lies one who wished to do good.' Yet when he died, on 2 October 1841, it was the memory of a tyrannical dictatorship which remained.

Honoré v never married and he had no children. He was succeeded by his younger brother Florestan. Few people could have been less equipped, or indeed less willing, to undertake the task which now confronted the new sovereign of Monaco. Still an infant at the time of the Revolution, he had been imprisoned with his divorced mother and it was she who had brought him up. Disregarding his literary tastes, she had compelled him to join the army, for which he felt the greatest repugnance. After an initial period of garrison duty in various parts of France, he accompanied the Grande Armée throughout the Russian campaign and was captured during the disastrous retreat. He remained a prisoner of war until the Allied victory of 1814.

When he married two years later, he showed his independence by choosing a commoner, a dancer called Caroline Gibert de Lametz, and they settled down to a quiet bourgeois life which was chiefly devoted to literary pursuits and the theatre. He enjoyed acting; he had appeared as a professional in eight different Paris theatres. 'I used to play young lovers,' he explained in later life. 'I was a favourite with audiences; they liked my voice and my cultured intonation . . . above all I looked a gentleman.' And a gentleman, not a ruler, was what he wished to remain. He had never so much as set foot in the principality. The prospect of exchanging the familiar comforts of his house in the Rue Saint-Guillaume for the anonymous grandeur of an isolated and unknown palace filled him with alarm. But there was no alternative.

His arrival at Monaco, on the evening of 21 November 1841, was greeted with joyful cries of 'Long live Florestan!' but this reassuring welcome was accompanied by other cries, less joyful ones, of 'Down with the *exclusive!*'* and on the very next day he was made aware of the prevailing temper of his subjects when the infamous Chapon was assaulted by an angry crowd in full view of the princely apartments. Terrified by the scene, Florestan abolished

* The local name for the bread monopoly.

the unpopular monopoly on the spot. In his eagerness to be left in peace, he was quite ready to make further concessions and suppress taxation altogether, no matter what the consequences. A sincere democrat, but ignorant of the most elementary economics, he failed to grasp that the suppression of one tax must lead to the creation of another if his revenue was not to be disastrously reduced. This he himself might not have minded, but his wife was more ambitious. 'Your father has given me a fine name,' Princess Caroline was writing to her son as early as 3 April 1842. 'In exchange I must see to it that his position remains the same and that his fortune is properly handled.' And see to it she did. She assumed her husband's sovereignty in all but name. He signed the various documents she drafted without even reading them.

Thus, of necessity, the feudal system was preserved; and for all his good intentions Florestan fell out of popular favour. Later, in a political comedy based on his reign called *Rabagas*, his existence at this time was aptly summarized. In it he is made to say:

I am an unfortunate little sovereign, crushed between two big neighbours who only hesitate as to the sauce with which they shall devour me . . . The treaty of 1817 forces me to put up with a Sardinian garrison at Menton, which protects me – till the first riot occurs. Then, it will support the rioters . . . I succeed my brother, Honoré v, and arrive here bubbling over with ideas of liberty, progress and reforms! I import two admirable English oil-mills and invite my subjects to send me their olives to grind. At once I am accused of arbitrary proceeding. Therefore I buy the olives and convert them into oil myself. Then the cry is raised that I am creating a monopoly. I suppress the mills and restore everything to its pristine state – I am accused of encouraging stagnation and routine . . . And from then on a sullen struggle begins between my subjects and myself, a struggle that has slowly developed into a state of ferocious hostility . . . All my acts are criticized, misrepresented and travestied! Take a few examples. I go for a walk – it is found that I have a lot of time to idle away. I do not go for a walk – then I am afraid of showing myself. I give a ball – I am accused of wild extravagance. I do not give a ball – I am mean and avaricious. I hold a review – I am attempting military intimidation. I do not hold a review – I am afraid and cannot trust the troops. Fireworks are let off on my birthday – I am wasting the people's money. I suppress the fireworks – then I do nothing for the people's amusement. I am in good health – that is because I am idle and take no trouble over public matters. I am in bad health – that is the result of debauchery. I build – wastefulness. I do not build – then what about the working classes? In fact I am no longer able to eat, sleep or keep awake. Everything I do is proclaimed detestable, and what I do not do gives even greater offence.

In 1847 and the early part of 1848 this 'ferocious hostility' manifested itself in a series of demonstrations in Menton and Roquebrune. The two communes, especially Menton with its rich lemon groves, were the only relatively productive areas in the principality, yet from time immemorial the Grimaldis had favoured the bare rock of Monaco at their expense. 'Menton and Roquebrune paid,' the saying went. 'Monaco profited.' Florestan did his best. He worked, negotiated, made promises, changed his mind and contradicted himself; in short, he hunted in every direction for a solution, and when none could be found he gave up in despair. On 10 March 1848 he handed all his power over to Prince Honoré-Charles, his thirty-year-old son. Ten days later he left for Paris, and never came back.

The ambitious young regent had been longing to try his administrative skill. But the opportunity had come too late. Openly encouraged by the Sardinian troops who were meant to suppress them, bands of armed rebels were already roaming through the streets of Menton. At Roquebrune angry demonstrators called for the dethronement of the Grimaldis, and on the same day – 20 March – both communes declared themselves free towns under the protection of the king of Sardinia. Only Monaco remained loyal to the prince.

The legal position of the two towns was disputed in the chancellories of Europe for the next six years. France in particular was vehement in protest against their virtual annexation. The regent himself never gave up the hope that the lost towns would return to their allegiance. Indeed he was so confident that in 1854 he resolved to visit Menton in the expectation that the people, disillusioned by Sardinian protection, would rise in his favour.

No sooner had his carriage drawn up outside the post office than he was recognized by some of his supporters and loudly acclaimed. It was six o'clock in the morning of 6 April. Within a few minutes a large crowd had gathered. They escorted him in triumph towards the town hall shouting: 'Long live the prince! Long live the Grimaldis! Down with the Sardinians!' Here the demonstrators came up against an armed contingent of the National Guard which was recruited from the opposing faction. A tussle ensued; the prince, conspicuous in his full-dress uniform, was severely man-handled. He might have suffered worse, for his supporters were outnumbered, had the mob not been dispersed by some Sardinian troops. They led him off to the barracks and locked him up, and there he remained until eleven o'clock that night. He was then transferred as a state prisoner to the fortress of Villefranche, from which he was not released – and only then after vigorous representations from Napoleon III – until four days later.

This adventure, if it accomplished nothing else, destroyed his hopes of ever recovering Menton and Roquebrune. But the loss of these two communes, to which he now had to reconcile himself, represented also the almost total loss of his income. Till 1848 the principality had been able to count on an average revenue of more than two hundred thousand francs. Over ninety per cent of this, however, was derived from the export tax on the lemons of Menton. Monaco itself had never yielded more than three thousand francs: not even enough for the regent's personal expenses. The prince had inherited his uncle's rather than his father's tastes. Prodigal by nature, he revelled in every kind of splendour and display. Yet Monaco was all that was left to him. Never before had he been so aware of the truth of the local dictum:

Monaco io sono
Un scoglio

Del mio non ho
Quello d'altrui non toglio
Pur viver voglio.

– 'I am Monaco, a stray rock. I have nothing of my own, I do not plunder the goods of others, and yet I want to keep alive.'

He too wanted to keep alive, to carry on the noble line of the Grimaldis, to perpetuate the evocative and resounding concatenation of titles held by the head of the family: Prince de Monaco, Duc de Valentinois, Marquis des Baux, Comte de Carladès, Baron du Buis, Seigneur de Saint-Rémy, Sire de Matignon, Comte de Torrigni, Baron de Saint-Lô, Baron de Hambye, Baron de la Luthumière, Duc d'Estoutville, Duc de Mazarin, Duc de Mayenne, Prince de Château-Porcien, Baron d'Altkirch, Marquis de Chilly, Baron de Massy, Marquis de Guiscard, Comte de Ferrette, Comte de Belfort, Comte de Thann, Comte de Rosemont, and Grandee of Spain.

But he was nearly bankrupt.

2

THE
SCENTED
ROCK

With the loss of Menton and Roquebrune, the principality had been reduced to one fifth of its former size and was now the smallest independent state in the world. It occupied an area no larger than Hyde Park in London, half that of Central Park in New York, and infinitely less than the Bois de Boulogne in Paris. Three distinct geographical features composed it: the Rock of Monaco itself, an oblong peninsula four hundred feet high, perched like a flower-bed in full bloom above the deep-blue sea; another slightly less abrupt promontory, forming the second side of a natural harbour; and a narrow strip of land connecting the two and sloping gently from the coast towards the foothills.

The horizontal surface of the rock was almost entirely occupied by the town, which consisted of the still partly ruined palace, three churches and five parallel streets intersected by a number of narrow lanes; and the whole was enclosed in ramparts superimposed on natural bastions of sheer cliff. In every cleft and on every ledge the Barbary figs grew in such profusion that when they flowered in July the naked stone was covered by a yellow curtain. Above the sun-bleached roof-tiles of the houses stood a clump of pines. There, some scattered palm-trees and an occasional larch and tamarisk, lentisk and oleander sprouted from the rare patches of earth in between. The rock afforded little for vegetation.

The promontory opposite was known as les Spélugues, from the Latin *speluncae*; which in this case were caves used for burial purposes. This was even harsher and, until 1828, completely barren. In that year, however, some convicts lent by the king of Sardinia were set to dumping earth for planting on the bare rock. The headland soon became an infirmary of crippled timber: the stony desert was dotted with stunted lemon trees and gnarled olives; and by the time Théodore de Banville saw them they looked so wild and venerable, especially the olives, that he found it difficult, he said, to believe that they had remained rooted to the earth all night. 'Surely at the first shadow of dusk, vanquished and changed these ancient Titans assume their ancient form and then, with menacing jaws agape, breathe fire through incandescent nostrils as they scale the neighbouring hills – there among the rocky wastelands and the raving torrents to engage in fierce and bloodstained orgies.' This steep and stony wilderness was unpopulated except for a few shepherds; across it twisted a rough pathway; and this, apart from the sea, was the only link between the principality and the rest of the world.

The narrow plain of the coast is called la Condamine – this name, common in the Midi, is a contraction of *campus domini* – and this Field of Our Lord was the only fertile part of the prince's estate. Protected from the north by a ridge of hills connecting the greater heights of Mont Agel and the Tête de Chien, it was a vast flower garden which stretched uninterruptedly from the base of the rock to the little ravine which divided it from the headland of the Spélugues. Behind it lay groves of lemon and orange and peach and apricot and almond interspersed with a profusion of eucalyptus and fig trees and olives.

Unaccustomed strangers, venturing too near in springtime and overcome by the combined scents of the violets and the jasmine, the roses and tuberoses and the eucalyptus and the orange blossom, remained rooted to the spot. The orange crop fulfilled two purposes. Picked at the New Year while it was still green, the fruit was either destined for export or, from the end of February, sold ripe and ready for eating; while the neroli – the oil extracted from the blossom – was used in the manufacture of scent or for drinking as orange-flower water. The lemon trees produced as many as twelve crops a year, and these were sold, depending on the quality of the fruit, for anything between five francs and thirty francs a thousand.

The other trees were so rich in fruit that everyone could make his own jam and still have enough left over to feed the cattle. It cost only the toil of picking; boatmen from Nice would never pay more than five or six francs for an entire boatload, and they were paying for the labour of loading rather than the value of the cargo. Children would shake the trees and stamp on the fruit for the sake of the stones; with almonds they were the adjuncts of one of their favourite games. Alongside the harbour, which is the ancient Port Hercules of the Romans and Phoenicians, the sheds were full of men cleaning lemons and packing crates; and three-mast sailing ships from as far off as America would put in and load up and sail away.

On the far side of the Spélugues stood one of the old mills which Prince Florestan had imported from England and which his son had restored to use. Apart from the houses clustering round, the few shepherds' huts on the headland and the harbour sheds, the only buildings outside the town walls were half a dozen isolated villas in the Condamine and a little chapel in the ravine dedicated to Sainte-Dévote, the patron saint of the principality.

Olive oil, scent, citrus fruit and dried figs: these represented Monaco's entire industry and commerce, and the revenue they provided sufficed the modest needs of the inhabitants. Their indolence and their lack of ambition were bywords. If you asked a Monégasque to work and he replied: '*Je ne me sens pas,*' it was useless to press him further. He didn't feel like it, and that was that.

But the prince's own requirements amounted to more than those of all his three thousand subjects combined. They were also far beyond anything that could be met by further exploitation – even supposing this to be possible – of the natural resources available. True, there was the climate. Monaco was so healthy that a single doctor could serve the entire population. The mountains behind the principality provided shelter from the northerly winds, yet the atmosphere was never oppressive and the purity of the air was assured by the great extent of the uninhabited mountain on one side and the expanse of sea on the other. The subsoil consisted mainly of rock shelving steeply to the water's edge, so natural drainage kept the whole area free from mist and damp; and since the Condamine was nothing but gardens and no sewers emptied in the port, the beautiful sands lower down where the galleys used to ground in ancient times were likewise free of impurities. Monaco had all the gifts of a natural health resort.

These gifts had already been noticed in the reign of Honoré v, when the idea of turning the estate into a spa had been suggested to him in an official memorial:

> Thanks to its splendid situation and wonderful climate the principality of Monaco should attract numerous visitors. It could become the refuge of large numbers of invalids, if only they could find comfortable accommodation and good cooking, and some of the distractions which a foreigner expects when he takes a holiday abroad. Such an establishment would indubitably be as profitable to its founders as to the country in general.

But despite the example of Nice, which was prospering even then from the number of wealthy foreigners who wintered there, Honoré had shrunk from the difficulties of the enterprise. Ever since Tobias Smollett had described the air of Nice as being 'agreeable to the constitution of those who labour under the disorders arising from weak nerves, obstructed perspiration, relaxed fibres, a vascidity of lymph, and a languid circulation', distinguished English invalids had struggled abroad from the fogs and cold of late autumn to return in April or remain there until they died. Villas and hotels had been built in the Croix de Marbre quarter of the town – they nicknamed it Newborough – and soon it became 'practically a suburb of London'. Smollett's cult for sea-bathing meanwhile – much to the initial surprise of the local doctors who knew that he was a consumptive and so prognosticated immediate death – had spread to other places on the coast until the Riviera had become a series of thriving resorts.

The most recent of these was Cannes. This unknown fishing village had neither pier nor harbour until its accidental 'discovery' in the autumn of 1834. Travelling to Genoa, Lord Brougham was halted at the Var, which was then the frontier, and informed that a *cordon sanitaire* had been established on account of an outbreak of cholera. Pending the arrival from Paris of the necessary permit to continue, he put up at the Hôtel de la Poste, which was the only inhabited house to the south of Mont Chevalier. He was so struck by the beauty of the neighbourhood that he resolved to buy a plot of land and build a house there. Many other English visitors followed his example, and the one-street village had become an established watering-place with a population of over five thousand.

If Cannes in a bare twenty years could develop to this extent, there seemed no reason why Monaco should not do likewise or even better. Honoré-Charles, deciding in favour of his uncle's rejected expedient, drew up a plan for the formation of a company to be known as La Société de Crédit de la Région Méditerranéenne, which would build a bathing establishment, a sanatorium and a number of private villas. But he was unable to raise the requisite capital of two million francs and no doubt the scheme would have been dropped had it not been for the enterprise of Princess Caroline; her concern for the welfare of the House of Grimaldi had not ceased with her departure from the principality. She knew that the Belgian and Rhineland spas owed most of their success to their casinos; she was particularly impressed by the growing prosperity of the landgraviate of Hesse-Homburg, a small sovereign state like Monaco itself. She therefore instructed her confidential man of affairs, a Parisian lawyer called Adolphe Eynaud, to visit Bad Homburg and find out under what conditions the grand duke had granted the concession there and how much money he made out of it.

He learnt that the grand duke's revenue from this source amounted to three hundred and fifty thousand francs, but this was 'only one among the advantages accruing to his treasury from the existence of the casino. More than two hundred thousand people visit the duchy annually, and spend money there like water.' Monaco, he added, could not count on such prosperity as that, but he advised the princess that a similar enterprise 'would undoubtedly prove a considerable source of revenue and be of the greatest benefit to the general interest as well as to that of Your Highness'. At the same time he suggested that gambling, though in reality the main object of the scheme, should appear to be only a sideshow: the policy of disguising a casino as a spa had been successfully adopted at Baden-Baden and at Wiesbaden and Homburg, where there were valuable mineral springs. Monaco's natural assets provided a similar ready-made façade, and so in March 1855 fresh plans were drawn up for a company under the innocuous name of La Société des Bains de Mer.

The idea of building a casino on the Riviera was not an original one. Six years earlier, in 1849, the municipality of Nice* had considered the question of granting a gambling concession, even though the Sardinian penal code imposed heavy penalties on games of hazard: any concessionaire or employee was liable to a fine and imprisonment from three months to one year, while any person detected gambling in a casino was liable to a fine of three hundred francs. It was improbable that the government would relax the law in favour of Nice, but the bare rumour of competition was enough to alarm the successful director of the Homburg casino, François Blanc.

To forestall any possible rival, Blanc immediately sought the concession for himself. Receiving no reply to his overture, he set out to make inquiries, and on his arrival he learnt that the concession had already been granted to a group of gamblers headed by a man called Phillippe. In order to 'checkmate the projects of these gentlemen', as he put it, he prolonged his journey as far as Turin, where he learnt that the municipality of Nice had not yet approached the government. He was also assured that consent to the illegal proposal would never be given; his attention was drawn to numerous articles attacking the project in the local press. This newspaper campaign was no surprise; he himself had reinforced it: a timely bribe had persuaded Amelio Bianchi-Giovini, the editor of *L'Opinione* and one of Italy's foremost publicists, to write a pamphlet opposing the concession, and when the question was eventually raised it had contributed to the government's renewed condemnation of gaming establishments within the kingdom of Sardinia. Shortly afterwards he was able to report back to Homburg that 'the Nice affair' had been completely abandoned.

* Nice was ceded to France by Sardinia in 1796, restored to Sardinia in 1814, and again ceded to France in 1860.

Kept informed by his numerous agents, he was one of the first to learn of the new project at Monaco. His opinion that it was 'so doubtful a venture that no one would undertake it' appeared at first to be justified. Largely thanks to intrigues at Nice – which Honoré-Charles rightly or wrongly attributed to the machinations of Blanc – prospective concessionaires were urgently dissuaded and no financial backing could be found. Even more decisive than these alleged machinations was the fear of Sardinian intervention. The treaty guaranteeing the sovereign independence of the principality had already been broken by the annexation of Menton and Roquebrune; it could well be broken again. The protection of Sardinia was a constant trammel and an embarrassment; Eynaud implored the prince to get rid of it. 'You will be ten times more respected,' he added, 'with a few gendarmes at the doors of your palace than with a whole regiment of Piedmontese guards; they would justly be regarded as your gaolers. You see the results of this protection in the matter of the casino. Nobody dares to come to terms.'

This was not quite accurate. Negotiations with a couple of financiers who seemed extremely anxious to come to terms were actually under way. Eynaud was merely apprehensive of anything that might curb their enthusiasm and, as neither of them had any experience of casino management, enthusiasm indeed appeared to be their only qualification. One of them, Napoleon Langlois, was a Paris businessman; his colleague, Albert Aubert, was a contributor to *Charivari*, the anti-monarchist paper made famous by Daumier's political and social caricatures. Serenely undeterred by the arguments that had dissuaded others and eager to start work at once, they submitted their plan for a palatial casino and all the accessory buildings. 'The engine that activates Monsieur Langlois's brain,' Eynaud observed, 'is getting up steam. He is at work on this business day and night.' He proved, however, to be Napoleonic only in name, and Eynaud was soon complaining of his changeable and excitable nature, which robbed him of the power of consecutive thought. Moreover nothing was known about the partners' financial status: nothing, that is, to Eynaud and the Grimaldis. But François Blanc had made careful inquiries and the result was extremely reassuring: Langlois could provide no more than two hundred thousand francs, most of them borrowed, and Aubert was penniless.

To the bankrupt reigning family, however, even unsupported promises seemed better than nothing, and since nobody else seemed willing to take up the matter an agreement was reached. On 26 April 1856 Prince Florestan granted Langlois and Aubert an exclusive concession for the construction of a bathing establishment, a large hotel and a number of villas, and sea and land communications between Monaco and Nice. The concessionaires were also authorized to provide amusements of every kind:

> notably balls, concerts, fêtes, games such as whist, écarté, piquet, faro, boston and reversi, as well as roulette with either one or two zeros, and trente-et-quarante with the *refait* or *demi-refait*,* all this at the discretion of the concessionaires, the whole being subject to the supervision of one or more inspectors or commissioners appointed by His Serene Highness.

On paper the capital of the company was to amount to three million francs; it was to be divided into six thousand shares, and at the end of two years a part of the net profits was to be paid into the prince's treasury. The granting of the concession was one of Florestan's last official acts. He died two months later, on 26 June 1856. His son succeeded him and reigned as Charles III.

Meanwhile Langlois and Aubert set to work and by the end of the year, in the hope of attracting possible shareholders, issued a prospectus couched in the most glowing language:

> The premises which the company has found are virtually ready. They consist of a large and beautiful villa commanding a magnificent view of the harbour, surrounded by a wonderful garden containing 2500 lemon and 2000 orange trees, as well as a large olive grove. A splendid mansion opposite the palace, belonging to His Highness the Prince of Monaco, has been placed at the disposal of the company. Finally, it has acquired an extensive tract of land known as les Spélugues, overlooking the harbour, 100,000 square metres in extent. A town of small villas in the

---

* For an explanation of these terms, see pp. 153 and 157.

English style could be built there, complete with orange, olive and lemon groves. This land can be bought at public auction for about 30 centimes a square metre, while that on the other side of the harbour is already worth more than ten francs the square metre.

These claims were exaggerated, to say the least. The 'large and beautiful villa' was merely the largest of those in the Condamine. The Villa Bellevue belonged to a Monsieur Arnoux; he attached little value to it and he was delighted to sell the property, together with 100,000 square metres of land, for sixty-four thousand francs. The land was completely wild and the premises far too small. Langlois and Aubert would never have bought them had not Princess Caroline decreed that the casino should be sited outside the town of Monaco. In view of this decree it was an idle boast to say that the splendid mansion opposite the palace was at the disposal of the company. It could never be used.

The land on the Spélugues had indeed been acquired, and for the ridiculously low price of twenty-two centimes the square metre, but the actual value could be judged from the fact that the mayor of Monaco had recently given away a large acreage of property there in exchange for a dinner for twelve. Meanwhile it was populated by lizards, rabbits and goats, and the only buildings were a few shepherds' huts. There was no sign of small villas in the English style. Nor, for that matter, was there any discernible preparation for the bathing establishment, the hotels and the communications with Nice, but these omissions were for the moment overlooked. Eynaud was more concerned that the principle of the casino should be accepted. He knew that the enterprise was open to attack, especially by those newspapers which were supported by the German spas with handsome advertisements. He therefore followed François Blanc's example and by the beginning of December he was able to report to the prince that of all the French papers only *L'Illustration* had indulged in hostile criticism. But he added the warning that success and increasing numbers of visitors would certainly lead to more serious attacks. It was impossible to muzzle the whole press.

Hostile newspapers might be silenced temporarily; there was also the threat of criticism on genuinely moral grounds. The Monaco establishment therefore had to be presented as an exception to the general run of gaming houses. It must have been this consideration which prompted the words of the court historian:

As a matter of principle, we do not approve of gaming houses, and the governments who suppress them act wisely. Established in large centres of the population, they constitute a permanent excitement, stimulating the spirit of cupidity, and encompass the demoralization and ruin of the unfortunate people who, attracted by the false hope of gain, press passionately round the green baize. But when such games are established far from large towns, and when the distance is such that the cost of the journey can only be met by rich foreigners, one may accord them the benefit of extenuating circumstances, for they do bring an element of prosperity to the native population, who themselves are severely excluded from the saloons.

To Langlois and Aubert these niceties mattered little. What did matter – and it was their one concern – was to start the roulette wheels spinning. Accordingly, on 14 November 1856, with the two biggest rooms hastily and scantily furnished, the entrance still incomplete, and the surroundings so filthy that the company directors were implored to clear everything away 'that might offend the eye or nose', the Villa Bellevue opened its doors to the public.

3

THE
UNSUCCESSFUL
PIONEERS

Langlois and Aubert were soon to learn the difficulties and hazards of a gaming establishment. 'The most luxurious casino in the world,' it has been pointed out, 'serving free banquets and fine wines, has no hope of success if it is hard to reach.' The Bellevue was anything but luxurious, it served no food or drink of any kind and it was wellnigh inaccessible.

Geography, the absence of roads and the prevalence of bandits had isolated Monaco for centuries. In fact the whole of the Riviera was avoided by early travellers and Nice itself was bypassed by all the established sea and land routes to Italy and the East. Until the rise of Marseilles, Aigues-Mortes had been the main French port for the central and eastern Mediterranean – it was here that the chronicler Jean de Joinville embarked with the crusaders of Saint Louis – while the overland route followed by the soldiers of the Fourth Crusade made its way to Venice by way of the Mont Cenis pass. Visitors to Monaco were few and seldom. Those who made the journey all spoke of its pitfalls and its perils. The rough seas of the area were a constant danger and, for fear of the Barbary pirates who regularly patrolled the Baie des Anges, vessels used to hug the coast under cover of the cannon at Nice or Antibes.

By land, Monaco could be reached only by a narrow footpath. The very idea made Madame de Sévigné tremble from head to foot when she heard that her beloved daughter Madame de Grignan had just travelled along it. 'You describe the perils of your journey only too well,' she wrote in June 1672. 'I don't understand them, that's to say I don't understand how one can expose oneself to them.' More than a hundred years later the same perils still haunted the path. It was aptly named the Corniche. In many places, according to Madame de Genlis, it was 'so narrow that one can hardly pass along it in single file: on the one side, huge rocks form a sort of battlement which seems to soar to the skies; on the other, one is right on the edge of five-hundred-foot precipices, at the base of which the sea, crashing against the rocks, makes a sound as sad as it is terrifying.'

Since then a proper carriageway had been built. It was started in 1808 by order of Napoleon, who wanted a good thoroughfare to Italy: but the engineer in command, a sapper officer by the name of Sigaud, who was impelled by a wholesome fear of English frigates, laid out his highway along the course of the old Corniche footpath instead of running it along the seashore. It took longer to complete than the whole Ligurian highway and the time and effort spent on cutting it out of the solid rock was so severely criticized by Napoleon that the wretched Sigaud committed suicide. But by April 1812 it had reached Roquebrune; here it joined the older road between Monaco and Menton which had been built under Prince Antoine I in 1720, thereby linking Nice to Genoa. It served its purpose in providing for the transport of the imperial troops from France to Italy, but since then it had been neglected. Roots of trees exposed by erosion and boulders dislodged by avalanches presented a constant hazard, yet the devious and dangerous road was still the only means by which the new casino could be reached overland from Nice.

An uncomfortable and antiquated vehicle, graced by the name of omnibus and carrying eleven passengers, made the journey once a day – in theory. On some days, for no apparent reason, it did not run at all. There was ample time to admire the landscape; the road ran more or less continuously uphill for twenty kilometres through a countryside that was almost totally uninhabited. An occasional cottage would show amidst the undergrowth of the ravines which sloped down to the sea. A solitary inn stood by the roadside at the top of the first long ascent. This was the Auberge des Quatres

Chemins or Trattoria degli Quatro Camini. The name appeared in both languages under a mural signboard on which Masséna, seated in full-dress uniform before a glass of wine, was a painted commemoration of the day in 1800 when the marshal – a mere corporal then – stopped here for a drink.

After this there was no building for two and a half hours until a lofty mass of ruins known as the Tower of Augustus announced the hamlet of La Turbie. Here the coachman would stop and point out a path winding down to the coast. 'Monaco is just below you,' he would say. 'If you don't want to drive all the way round by Roquebrune, you can make your way straight down on foot.' Monaco appeared deceptively close from this height, and the unwary, anxious to avoid an additional hour's drive, would usually follow the coachman's advice on the assumption that the direct descent would take no more than fifteen minutes or so. It took much longer.

Approach by sea was equally erratic. There was no regular boat service and the one extremely unsafe-looking steamer, like the omnibus, would sometimes not start out at all. Allegedly under repair, she would remain in Nice harbour for weeks on end. An additional obstruction beset the sea route in the shape of passport formalities. From the tourist point of view Monaco was still a desert. A small house near the casino had been converted into a hotel, which provided board but no bed. The only place to stay overnight was the mansion opposite the palace, where officers of the French garrison used to be billeted in the eighteenth century. It now bore the grandiose name of Hôtel de Russie, and a few sparsely furnished rooms were available. Visitors from Nice had to return there every evening and the double journey, combined with the general sordidness of the place, failed to attract the kind of clientèle the company had hoped for. The quality of the gamblers at the Bellevue could be judged by the number of counterfeit coins and forged banknotes which appeared at the tables within the first few days, and it was soon discovered that someone had been tampering with the roulette wheel, though whether the intention was to cheat the bank or to cast suspicion on the directors, no one could tell.

Despite the modest level of the gambling – the maximum stake was fixed at the comparatively low sum of three thousand francs – the casino won 41,776 francs during the first two months of its existence. Its greatest daily win on a single day – 22 January 1857 – was 15,958 francs; its greatest loss – on 3 February – was 7,101 francs. Even a small loss like this was enough to alarm the management, who promptly reduced the bank's reserves at the trente-et-quarante table to ten thousand francs and at the roulette table to five thousand.

By 4 March it was clear that the two concessionaries were nearing the end of their financial resources. Their hope that the shares would find a ready sale once the company was floated had not been fulfilled. Out of two thousand shares, with a nominal value of one million francs, only 417 had been taken off their hands – mainly by Langlois himself – and these had produced a total sum of 208,565 francs: barely enough to meet current expenses. Far from helping the prince with their enterprise, Langlois and Aubert were now obliged to seek help from him to keep the enterprise going. In revealing their plight they pointed out the dangers of liquidation, which, they insisted, must at all costs be avoided for everybody's sake. For if the company were to change hands, the shareholders, however few, would have to be paid back – and this had become impossible. An appalling scandal loomed; its consequences would have been incalculable and the prince was as eager to avoid it as the partners; but his only remedy was to allow them to continue.

Between 15 and 20 March only one visitor entered the casino, and won two francs; on the 21st two more arrived, and lost two hundred and five. Nevertheless, when the accounts were made up for the first quarter of 1857, it was found that the casino had made a profit of fifty-four thousand francs. But the remainder of the year showed a steady loss. On 7 December the government commissioner reported the same dearth of players. Only two had appeared since 30 November, and they lost 640 francs. 'Though the rooms were opened for play fourteen times during the week,' he reported a little later, 'gambling took place only five times. Neglected publicity and lack of communications with Nice are to blame.'

It was becoming evident that Langlois and Aubert would never

make the Bellevue pay. Fortunately for them, a clause in their contract allowed them, with the prince's consent, to transfer their
concession to a reputable successor. They professed to have found
one in the person of a certain Froissard de Lilbonne; the whole
enterprise and its embarrassing liabilities were accordingly transferred. Lilbonne persuaded the prince to allow him to re-establish
the casino in the Hôtel de Russie, in the hope that the neighbourhood of the palace would provide glamour. But his capabilities
were never put to the test; before the year was out he had sold the
concession to a man called Pierre Auguste Daval, whom he
described as 'a capitalist of unquestioned solvency'. The new
concessionaire had been a member of the famous Paris club
Frascati's, which had been put out of business by the 1837 abolition of public gambling in France. His capital, mostly borrowed
from a lady friend, was barely enough to cover the purchase price
of 1,208,000 francs. Moreover he appeared to be entirely unknown
in the business world. Eynaud, who had not been informed of the
transfer, was justifiably apprehensive.

Daval proved as disappointing as the others. The casino now
consisted of a single gloomy room with two tables for roulette and
one for trente-et-quarante. His croupiers were unemployed Nice
waiters and broken-down gamblers – *décavés*, as they were called –
who had lost all their money in the clandestine gambling dens of
the town. There was a small and needy clientèle of bankrupts and
exiles from Homburg and Baden-Baden; none of the rich habitués
of these places could put up with the squalor of Monaco. Nothing
had been done to improve communications and none of the
improvements had been carried out, except for pulling down the
shepherds' huts to make room for the eventual casino. On 13 May
1858 the foundation stone of this future establishment was actually
laid, and Daval showed a certain dash in his choice of the hundred
and fifty guests he invited to the ceremony. The convoy, which
included a best-selling novelist called Alphonse Karr, Baron de
Bazancourt, the famous duellist, the sculptor Adolphe Megret and
Amaury Duval, the painter, started out from Nice in smart landaus
decked out with ribbons in the Monégasque and French colours.
They halted for refreshment at La Turbie and finally – white with

dust and roasted by the blazing sun – drew up outside the Hôtel de Russie, where Daval, dressed in a frock coat and white gloves and a starched shirt-front adorned with a diamond the size of a decanter stopper, conducted them into the banquet. The aptly chosen menu with its gambling connotations heavily underlined was printed on vellum:

HORS D'OEUVRES
Radis *noirs*
Huitres à la *douzaine*

ENTREES
Carrés de veau à la casserole
Gigots découpés en *transversales*

ROTI
Pigeons sur canapés
Petits poulets de *gain*

ENTREMETS
Pièces montées
Rateaux de Savoie

DESSERTS
Fruits étagés en *colonnes*
Cerises de la famille de la *guigne*

VINS
Toute une *série* de vins *rouges*

LIQUEURS
Kummel *double zéro*
Bols avec eau à la ver-*veine*

Nota. Les convives peuvent se placer par table de *trente-et-quarante*. Chaises ou fauteuils à *roulettes*, au choix. Vestiaire avec *numéros* d'ordre.

Prince Charles, who was already afflicted by an incipient blindness which two years later was to become total, joined them at the end of the meal. Toasts were drunk to the past and present Grimaldis, to Monaco and its inhabitants, and above all to the success of the casino and the splendid projects of the new director.

But the splendid projects failed to materialize. As the walls of the new building rose from its rocky foundation, the rock itself began to give way. The workmen complained that their pay was in arrears. The architect, Godineau de la Bretonneraie, soon became so disgusted that he packed his bags and left not only Monaco but Europe; he eventually became a cabinet minister in the government of the Negus of Abyssinia. Daval meanwhile, instead of contributing to the prince's treasury, ran deeper and deeper into debt; by August Eynaud was writing to him with some asperity: 'His Highness will not and cannot allow matters to go on as they are at present. The employees have got to be paid and proper accounts must be kept.' But Daval had no money, even for his most pressing needs. Eynaud's indignation was understandable, for the prince's own financial position was still so precarious that for a time he was almost tempted to sell the principality to the emperor of Russia. But nothing came of it and the fate of Monaco continued to depend on the prospects of the casino.

These prospects were now further jeopardized by the international situation. On 10 December Cavour and Napoleon III concluded a treaty with the purpose of driving the Austrians out of northern Italy and by the beginning of 1859 war seemed inevitable. On 18 January the steamer *Malfatamo* put into Monaco to transfer the Sardinian garrison to Turin. Freed from this restraint, the Monégasques began to voice their discontent. Using the unsatisfactory progress of the casino as a pretext, they marched on the palace and proclaimed the revolution, though it was not at all clear with what purpose. Whatever it was, on 6 February an armed mob advanced on the Rock. The National Guards were quickly mustered and the gates of the old town closed; and when cannon were brought to bear upon the insurgents they lost heart and surrendered.

Incidents like this, combined with blunders in management, were no help to the casino's balance sheet, which soon showed a deficit of 1,262,000 francs. Daval was proving even more incompetent than his predecessors. Fortunately it was not hard to get rid of him, for it so happened that the Duc de Valmy, a rich and respected grandson of Marshal Kellerman, had become keenly interested in buying the concession, and on 28 May it was transferred from Daval to François Lefebvre, the chairman of the Valmy syndicate. Daval died in penury a few years later in a Marseilles hospital.

The efforts of Lefebvre and his associates meanwhile were considerably hampered by the outbreak of war. The principality sided openly with France, communications between Nice and Monaco were disrupted and the new concessionaires decided to close things down for the duration. They took advantage of these two months to find better premises for the casino. The headquarters of the Sardinian garrison had occupied one of the largest houses in the town: the Villa Gabarini – known locally as the Maison du Général – stood at the eastern end of the Rue de Lorraine. It was the obvious choice. The gaming tables were installed and when the war ended, with the defeat of Austria, the new casino opened its doors.

During the first ten weeks the tables made an average profit of a thousand francs a day, but at the beginning of the New Year one player alone was so consistently lucky that the returns for the first week of 1860 showed a loss of forty thousand francs. Lefebvre proved to be a timorous and parsimonious man and this comparatively minor setback was enough to upset him; when the casino continued to lose steadily during the remainder of January, he became panic-stricken. He was haunted by the memory of his predecessors' failure and this obsession, combined with his inexperience of casino management, drove him to measures which could only make matters worse. Whenever, for instance, the bank's resources at the trente-et-quarante table were exhausted by an unfavourable run of luck, instead of replenishing them he would close the table for the day. It prevented him from recouping the losses, made a bad impression and kept reputable gamblers away.

There was little enough to attract them in any case; Lefebvre's cheese-paring methods affected the whole enterprise. The gaming rooms were ill-equipped, badly lit and shoddily furnished. As he grudged the price of having the ballroom painted, it was only whitewashed – an economy which led to a ruinous display of disguising palms and flowers when at last he decided to give a fête by way of promotion. Similar methods bedevilled communications between Nice and Monaco. Hoping to set up a regular omnibus service, he entrusted it to a coachman called Joseph; but the vehicle and the harness were wretched, there were not enough horses and Joseph himself refused to drive because he was perched too high. When a rival firm offered a four-in-hand with magnificent trappings and a liveried coachman, Lefebvre, though tempted, recoiled from the expense. In any case the fifty-franc price of the journey overland was too dear for the class of gambler who went to gamble at Monaco; most of them preferred to come by sea.

'Weather permitting', a ramshackle old steamer called the *Palmaria* now plied daily to and fro between Nice and Monaco. The fifteen-mile voyage took two hours but the service was often disrupted by the captain's reluctance to sail if the sea looked rough. He would delay in Nice long after the scheduled departure time in the hope of a couple of extra passengers and would start back long ahead of time. It was quite a common thing to see people come running down to the Condamine waving handkerchiefs and shouting to him to wait.

In spite of all this, by March 1860 the bank had won more than one hundred and fifty thousand francs. Even taking into account the reverses suffered in January, it maintained its thousand francs daily profit. Yet Lefebvre still failed to see the wood of the overall gain for the trees of an occasional loss and flinched at outlay, although the lack of the promised amenities was persistently undermining the casino's prospects. As the government commissioner inconsequently reported, 'The disappointment of those coming to Monaco is so great that by this time everybody knows there are no comfortable hotels, no bathing facilities, no amusements of any kind and that nobody goes there now at all.'

It was not quite true. Gamblers came, but they were not the sort that could afford expensive hotels. Many of them could not even afford the minimum two-franc stake; they would resort to the nearby Café du Soleil, and play cards for a few sous a hand until one of them had made enough to venture into the gaming rooms. Meanwhile the weary croupiers would stroll about outside smoking cigarettes or climb the battlements to scan the Nice road by tele- scope for more remunerative clients. They rarely appeared, but Lefebvre still did nothing to attract more. He put no advertise- ments in the press, paid his staff so badly that the best had resigned, and made no attempt to build the stipulated hotels and villas. There were the rudiments of a bathing establishment in the Condamine and the construction went on, but at the slightest reverse work stopped on these two projects for days at a time.

It was soon clear that this short-sighted policy was prompted by lack of cash as well as by parsimony and inexperience. By Novem- ber, having frittered away all the money advanced by his partners, Lefebvre was compelled to transform the enterprise into a limited company. Like his predecessors, he tried to find prospective share- holders but met with as little success. His temperament and his incapacity were becoming well known. The company's balance sheet for 1860 showed a loss of 80,434 francs.

By the treaty of Turin of 24 March 1860, Sardinia had rewarded France for her participation in the recent victory over Austria by the cession of Nice and Savoy, but there had been no mention of Menton and Roquebrune; the two 'free towns' were still in their former anomalous position. The provisional governor of the county of Nice therefore organized a plebiscite to determine whether the inhabitants favoured annexation to France or re- integration with Monaco under a French protectorate. Out of an electorate of one thousand one hundred and twenty, eight hundred and eighty-nine voted in favour of union with France. This was a serious blow to Prince Charles, who forthwith protested against the illegality of the elections, but he was eventually persuaded by Napoleon III to accept the situation and on 2 February 1861 he signed a treaty surrendering his claim to Menton and Roquebrune in perpetuity. But the French government undertook to pay him four million francs to make up for the consequent loss of revenue. The prince also stipulated – no doubt on Eynaud's advice – that France should build a carriage road along the coast between Nice and Monaco while it still maintained the existing Corniche road. Finally, and most important of all, France confirmed her recognition of the independence and sovereignty of the prince's remaining territory.

Monaco was thus rid for-ever of the Sardinian protectorate and of the danger of Sardinian intervention in the gaming concern. Instead of taking advantage of this, Lefebvre persevered in his myopic tactics and in April, through excess of caution, he took the inexcusable step of introducing a second zero at the roulette tables. Although the odds against their winning were higher now, gamblers continued to come – Monaco, after all, was the only casino in southern Europe – and all through the summer the casino continued to show an average daily profit of a thousand francs. This could have been greatly multiplied had Lefebvre risen to the occasion, but he had neither the money nor the imagination. His sole initiative was the offer of a free site on the Spélugues to anyone undertaking to build a villa there, but no one took advantage of his offer.

Lefebvre's disinclination to improve the amenities of Monaco once more impelled the prince to remind him of his obligations: unless the casino were completed by the end of the following year the concession would be withdrawn. Considering the prolonged and severe tax that had been imposed on the prince's patience, this demand was hardly unreasonable. The establishment of gaming rooms in Monaco had not saved his principality from dismemberment; nor had it contributed a franc to his treasury; yet lack of an alternative solution compelled him to persevere with the project. But, strengthened by the payment of the four million francs, and with a correspondingly lessened need of the casino as a source of revenue, he could afford to adopt a more intransigent attitude.

It was impossible for the concessionaires to fulfil the terms of his ultimatum. But it was likewise impossible to liquidate the company entirely, for by this time too many people were involved. A compromise was reached. Lefebvre resigned his position and four of the principal shareholders formed a provisional committee to carry on business while the company was being reorganized. In the meantime the Duc de Valmy, as the largest shareholder, set out to find someone with the capacity to set the enterprise on its feet. No one without considerable experience and financial backing was likely to be interested in the deal. But there was a man with all the necessary qualifications, the one who had first applied for the concession – François Blanc, the highly successful director of Homburg. The duke decided to approach him.

4

THE
BLANC
BROTHERS

François Blanc and his twin brother Louis were born on 12 December 1806 in the little Provençal village of Courthezon. Their father, a poor tax-collector, died shortly before their birth, leaving their mother to bring them up. There were barely sufficient means to pay for their education and give them a small capital to start them in life.

The two brothers, who were similar in appearance as well as in character and disposition, were too ambitious and enterprising to stay at home. For some years they moved from one town to another, putting their hands to a variety of jobs. All business connected with finance and banking attracted them, but they were often forced to undertake more menial tasks, and at one time François worked as a waiter in a third-class Paris restaurant. With the characteristic weakness for manipulating figures which is common to many capitalists, he experimented with the accounts and was dismissed. His capital was now twenty francs. Confident in their financial flair and their aptitude for cards, the brothers turned to gambling as a career; they played écarté and baccara in the humble gaming houses that were still to be found in all the larger French towns and they occasionally risked their winnings on the stock exchange. It was a nerve-wracking life, but they had soon made enough money to start in business on their own and in 1834 they opened a small enterprise in Bordeaux. Though it was graced by the name of Bank it throve mainly by speculation on the rise and fall of government stocks.

Successful speculation, they had learnt, depended chiefly on exclusive information, and they had made a careful study of the means of communication employed by rival bankers. Since wireless telegraphy, and even the telephone, had not yet been invented, these means were elementary and sometimes ingenious. The Rothschilds used carrier pigeons to keep abreast of the movements of important securities; others arranged with millers to relay information by signals from one windmill to the next, but no method was as reliable and efficient as the *télégraphe aérien* invented by the Chappe brothers in 1794. Signalling stations were erected at convenient intervals and each was manned by an observer with a telescope who semaphored any message he received to the next station in line.

Paris and Bordeaux had been connected by this optical telegraph since 1823, and the Blancs were quick to realize that it offered the only means by which they could forestall their rivals. But the apparatus was a government monopoly, and only employed for the transmission of official news. This restriction was a serious obstacle, but to men like the Blancs it was a challenge. They first attempted to infiltrate the system by bribing a telegraph employee in Paris to insert an ostensible error in an official coded message to indicate a rise or fall in the *rentes*, as the government stocks were termed. Unfortunately for them this error was spotted by another employee in Tours, whose task was to check and correct all official communications, so that when the signal reached Bordeaux it contained no message for the twins. Undaunted, they next suborned a telegraphist stationed at Tours, who was thus able to insert the necessary error in a message after it had been checked. This method was slower than the original scheme, for their source in Paris had to fall back on the ordinary postal service to contact their agent in Tours. In spite of this they received the stock exchange prices more quickly than any of their rivals and were thus enabled to sell or buy accordingly. In the course of two years their operations yielded a profit of a hundred thousand francs.

Early in 1837, however, one of the telegraph employees involved in the conspiracy fell mortally ill, and in a fit of remorse on his deathbed he revealed every detail of the conspiracy. The Blanc brothers were charged with corruption and, on 11 March, brought to trial. They declared that they had had no criminal intention and pointed out, with some justification, that all bankers used similar means. They cited the Rothschilds as an example and slyly added: 'And you know, gentlemen, that Monsieur de Rothschild is generally esteemed, received at court and very popular.' They admitted that their own method had been technically fraudulent, but insisted that it had done no harm to the ordinary investor. 'No one was robbed,' they claimed. They were found guilty, but there was no established penalty for this particular offence, and this lack of precedent was eagerly seized upon by their counsel. 'Let us not invent penalties,' he advised the court, 'but content ourselves with those already contained in the legal code.' They got off scot-free, and were only ordered to pay the relatively small costs of the case, but their reputation in Bordeaux was ruined and so, with the greater part of their profits still intact, they moved to Paris and devoted themselves once more to gambling.

Public gambling had been a popular pastime in Paris ever since the reign of Henri IV, who himself set the fashion for it though he was not a skilful player and is said to have been 'greedy of gain, timid in high stakes, and ill-tempered when he lost'. There were then forty-seven licensed gaming houses in the capital, but these were all suppressed in the next reign by Louis XIII who preferred chess. But gambling came back into fashion under Louis XIV, when card-playing and games of chance were reintroduced at Court by Cardinal Mazarin in 1648. The vogue spread to every class of society.

One of the favourite games at this time was a rudimentary form of roulette of Italian origin called hoca. This game, which was introduced by Mazarin himself, was so prodigiously favourable to the bank – the players having only twenty-eight chances against thirty – that many people were ruined and the Paris Parlement consequently outlawed it as a capital offence. This law had little effect. 'The game of hoca is prohibited in Paris under penalty of death,' Madame de Sévigné wrote to her daughter in 1676, 'and yet it is played at court.' Basset, at which Madame de Montespan once lost four million pistoles at a sitting, was another popular game; it was known in England as faro or pharaoh and was supposedly invented by a Venetian noble. Yet another, called reversi, a card game at which the player with the fewest tricks wins, was constantly played in the royal apartments for two pistoles* a hundred points, a stake at which two or three thousand louis could be won or lost in an evening. It was no doubt excesses of this kind that eventually prompted the king to make the playing of such games punishable by a fine of a thousand livres and six months' imprisonment. But the very severity of these penalties defeated their object, for they could not be equitably imposed. Gambling spread, and by the time Louis xv ascended the throne 'three fourths of the nation thought of nothing else'.

During the regency of the Duc d'Orléans many of the houses of the great nobles were virtually *tripots* or gambling dens and, according to Horace Walpole, at least a hundred and fifty people of the highest quality lived on the play which took place in their houses. Gaming rooms were also to be found in the privileged mansions of ambassadors and representatives of foreign courts, where police officers were forbidden entry. Others were furtively established in premises that did not enjoy such diplomatic immunity, and here the nature of the play could be inferred from the name – *enfers* – by which, for the first time, they came to be known. It soon became evident that no law would ever put a stop to these hells; the dice were often loaded, the cards marked, and the public was robbed in a score of different ways. Determined to control what he could not abolish, the chief of police, Gabriel de Sartine, authorized the opening of licensed and supervised houses for a number of games, of which roulette was the most conspicuous.

The roulette wheel was then a comparatively new device and its invention has often been attributed to Pascal. From his very birth, according to Michaud's *Biographie Universelle*, he devoted himself to researches concerning combinations in games of hazard and he conducted a lengthy correspondence on the subject with his fellow-mathematician, Pierre de Fermat, which laid the foundations for the mathematical theory of probability. It wasc ertainly Pascal who

* A ten-franc coin, worth half a louis.

coined the word 'roulette', but as used by him it referred to a trochoid or cycloid, that is to say the curve traced in space by a point on a rolling circle. It had nothing to do with gambling.

The fundamental principle of roulette in the present-day sense must have come into existence as soon as man had progressed sufficiently to make wheels and organize games of chance. A primitive version of the game may have been devised by turning a chariot on its side, painting the upper wheel in different colours and using a spear stuck in the ground as a pointer. Fortuna, the Roman goddess of chance, was often represented holding a wheel or standing on a ball, and the wheel of fortune of the later Middle Ages was marked with numbers corresponding to a man's age. These essential elements – the wheel, the ball and the numbers – together with Pascal's theories on the law of probabilities formed the basis for the mathematically accurate gambling instrument that came into being towards the end of the seventeenth century.

The apparently haphazard distribution of the numbers round the circumference was in fact devised so that on either side of the zero there should be an equal amount of *pairs* and *impairs*, reds and blacks, and *passes* and *impasses*.* On the sloping disc surrounding the wheel obstacles were introduced so that when the ball was projected round it, its subsequent movement could not be dictated by deliberate interference. The wheel spun easily and took some time to stop – a good modern wheel can be made to spin for at least twelve minutes – thus allowing gamblers enough time to place their bets. Roulette came to be recognized as the most honest form of gambling that could be established, and it found special favour in the eyes of the police authorities. As Diderot and d'Alembert observed in the Encyclopaedia: 'At roulette players may risk their money in complete security.'

Other games were also allowed on licensed premises and in 1818, besides nine tables for roulette and seven for trente-et-quarante, there was still a table devoted to passe-dix, one of the most ancient games of chance, which is said to have been played by the Roman soldiers for the seamless garment of Christ. Another was devoted to craps, the original of the game which was later

* For an explanation of these terms see p. 148.

reintroduced to Europe via America under the same name. There was also a table for hazard, a more complicated version of the Franco-American game; and another for biribi, a form of roulette played with seventy numbers. These twenty tables were distributed among nine houses in various parts of Paris and yielded an annual profit of nearly two million francs. The houses were supervised by inspectors and croupiers, who were in turn subject to the control of other officials, and they were eminently respectable, especially those in the Palais Royal. At No. 36 no woman was admitted and strong drink was forbidden. No. 50 was patronized chiefly by the royalist party; and during the Allied occupation of Paris, Marshal Blücher was a constant visitor at No. 154, where he played for very high stakes and expressed his dissatisfaction because the house rules did not allow him to put down more than ten thousand francs at a time. On Sundays No. 154 was crowded beyond endurance, and No. 113 had a sinister reputation for suicides.

All these establishments, besides countless illegal *tripots* and *maisons de bouillotte*, were still functioning when the Blanc brothers arrived in Paris in the spring of 1837. At that time the two most fashionable were Frascati's and the Salon des Etrangers. They were also the most exclusive, but the twins had no difficulty in obtaining admission: they were sponsored by a Bordeaux acquaintance called Benazet who was then the farmer-general of all the metropolitan houses of play. From Benazet they also learnt what enormous profits could be derived from running an establishment devoted to roulette and trente-et-quarante. But the fate of such establishments in France was already decided. After the revolution of July 1830 had brought Louis Philippe to the throne, there had been a great outcry against the evil company which the proximity of gambling houses attracted to the Palais Royal, and a law was passed to abolish all public gaming after 1 January 1838. The Blanc brothers had arrived too late to set up in business themselves and for the time being had to be content with the comparatively modest sums they won as clients.

On the last day of legal gambling – Sunday, 31 December 1837 – there was such a rush to the tables that additional police had to be summoned to maintain law and order. The Salon, which usually opened only from eleven o'clock onwards, opened its doors two hours earlier. At Frascati's the rooms were already so thronged by ten o'clock that the doors had to be closed in the faces of the crowd outside. No. 113 lived up to its sinister reputation to the very end, when a workman killed himself on leaving.

Like any other measure of suppression, the abolition of licensed gaming houses ultimately defeated itself: as Sartine had realized, it led to uncontrolled and clandestine gambling. Furthermore the charitable institutions were deprived of the revenue from the tax which the law imposed on gambling profits. In 1837 alone this had amounted to over a million francs, and while other countries continued to benefit from the proceeds of the tables, the French government lost an annual sum of six million francs derived from gaming licences. Thus, in the words of the satirist Joseph Méry:

> *Nous avons détruit*
> *Frascati, le Salon, le coin de Marivaux,*
> *Pour enrichir les bains de trois pays rivaux.**

The watering-places most enriched were those in the Rhineland. Gambling had taken place on a modest scale ever since pump-rooms had been established there. French gamblers now began to flock to these resorts, whose fortunes were further enhanced by the diaspora of the Paris managers and staff. Benazet himself transferred his skill and experience to the Konversationshaus at Baden-Baden; the Kursaal at Wiesbaden was taken over by his colleague Chabert; Dupressoir settled at Ems; and others departed for Schwalback, Kissingen, Pyrmont, Spa and Aix-la-Chapelle.

The Blanc brothers were determined to follow their example. They were now thirty-five years old and their experience had convinced them that they could make a fortune out of gambling, not by playing themselves but by holding the bank. It was beyond their means, however, to buy a concession at any of the established spas. Their funds would not stretch to the large sums demanded by the Belgian authorities and the rulers of the more prosperous German states.

* i.e. Belgium, Germany and Switzerland.

They therefore moved to Luxembourg, where they organized a private club and where François, incidentally, formed an attachment with a woman who later bore him two sons. But the club was only a temporary measure until they could embark on a more ambitious scheme, and eventually they decided to try their luck in Hesse-Homburg.

It was the very insignificance of this diminutive landgraviate which dictated their choice. Not much more than a hundred square miles in area, its three thousand inhabitants were miserably poor. The capital was little more than a village consisting of the landgrave's castle and the few hundred ancient houses clustering round it. There was a mineral spring, but, apart from a small pump-room known as the Brünnensälchen, it had not been exploited for lack of funds. The single inn, called the Adler, catered for a few Frankfurt families who came to drink the waters and live cheaply during the heat of the summer. There were no hotels or gardens or amusements of any kind.

The Blanc brothers decided that if they supplied these amenities and developed Homburg as a spa, they might be granted a gambling concession on more favourable terms than they were likely to find elsewhere. Their conclusion was to prove correct. On 14 July 1840 they wrote to the landgrave requesting an audience, and two weeks later they signed an agreement with him whereby they were to build a kursaal or casino costing at least one hundred thousand gulden.* It was to be completed by 1842, when it would become the property of the landgrave, who would lease it to them until 1871, together with a concession for gambling, at a yearly rental of three thousand gulden for the first ten years, six thousand for the second decade, and ten thousand for the third. In the meantime a deposit of twenty-five thousand gulden was to be paid, and permission was granted for gaming tables in a room at the Adler or in the Brünnensälchen while the casino was being built.

Eager though they were to begin at once, the Blanc brothers were determined to set the enterprise on a firm footing. A Homburg publicity campaign was launched, an orchestra was engaged, horses and donkeys were bought, concerts and fêtes were organized, and

* The gulden or florin was then worth about 8p, or 20 cents.

facilities for every kind of sport were arranged, including hunting. Lavish plans were drawn up for the casino and the foundation stone was laid with appropriate ceremony in May 1841. It was only after the completion of these costly preliminaries that the two brothers, assisted by a former croupier from Frascati's, finally set up their gaming tables in the Brünnensälchen.

Even before they had made any profits at all, they decided to grant certain very definite advantages to the public by equipping their roulette wheel with one zero instead of two and introducing only a *demi-refait* at trente-et-quarante. This measure reduced their own prospects of gain, but they hoped it would attract high-staking gamblers from the Rhineland spas where these advantages were not to be found. Their boldness was rewarded, for within a year the number of visitors to Homburg more than doubled, and though the receipts from the gaming tables increased proportionately they still barely covered the cost of setting up the spa from scratch. There were houses, hotels and *pensions* to be built, streets, gardens and promenades laid out, and the new casino to be completed. All the profits were ploughed straight back into the business and for some time the Blancs were permanently threatened by a shortage of ready money. At one stage they found themselves unable to pay the builders' weekly wages and they were forced to approach the government of Hesse-Homburg for a loan of one hundred thousand gulden, but this was readily granted in view of the healthy state of their account books and their manifest desire to honour the terms of their contract.

Heralded by advertisements in the leading French newspapers and celebrated by a banquet and a ball which the landgrave himself graced with his presence, the opening of the new casino took place on 17 August 1843. The sumptuous gaming room, with its walls covered with dove-grey silk and its chairs gleaming with gilt and morocco leather, was thronged not only by the local gentry but also by many foreign visitors. Thanks to the Blancs' judicious publicity campaign, the attractions of Homburg were no longer unknown and the success of the young spa seemed to be assured.

And so it was, to the confusion of observers who disapproved of gambling. One of its sternest critics, the biographer Karl August

Vernhagen von Ense, denounced it as 'a nest of vagabonds, adventurers, cut-purses and disreputable women'. He deplored the presence of the Elector of Hesse, 'stooped over the table, gambling all through the day, peering at the cards and pushing his gold backwards and forwards – a revolting sight'. This sovereign prince did indeed lose vast sums to the Blanc brothers, but they were nothing compared to the losses of certain Russian aristocrats. They played incessantly and wildly, and the most notorious of them was Countess Sophie Kisselev, to be later immortalized as the 'Grandmother' in Dostoevsky's *Gambler*, the novel which he based on his own experiences at 'Roulettenburg'. Aged, infirm, and unable to move without the support of a servant, she would sit at play, day in, day out, in a specially upholstered chair, surrounded by hypnotists and spiritualists and the dishonest inventors of systems who styled themselves professors. It took immense losses to destroy her superstitious belief in these parasites. Thanks to her and her compatriots, in three years the Blancs had repaid the hundred thousand gulden they had borrowed and, by turning the enterprise into a public company, freed themselves of personal liabilities while retaining control. By 1847 there were five thousand visitors, not counting birds of passage, and a profit of 273,514 gulden. Hotels, villas and bath-houses had sprung up, trade and industry flourished and everybody, from the landgrave down to the least of his subjects, shared in the mounting prosperity.

But, like Monaco, Homburg suffered from the 1848 revolution. Inspired by the changes in France, the Germans replaced the old Diet of Frankfurt with a National Assembly. The new parliament declared public gambling illegal, ordered the closure of casinos and revoked concessions. As this decree meant ruin for both the Blancs and the landgrave, they quite simply decided to disregard it, and gave way only after a body of troops had been sent to enforce it. Even then the twins refused to admit defeat: within three weeks they had reopened the gaming rooms in the guise of a private club where only members and their guests could be admitted; but each member had the right to introduce his own family and his friends. Needless to say, it was not difficult to become a member and there were almost as many gamblers as before.

Soon, however, the National Assembly was dissolved, all its decrees were revoked, and lawful public gaming was resumed. But the temporary suspension had imposed a strain on the Blancs' nerves as well as on their resources. Exhausted and emaciated by worry, Louis Blanc fell seriously ill, and the whole responsibility for the enterprise devolved upon his brother. François was quite capable of carrying on by himself, but was often compelled to leave Homburg. He was kept busy organizing publicity campaigns in Paris, persuading the railway companies to speed up their lines to Germany, and investigating the possibility of a rival casino opening in Nice. During one of these absences, while his ailing brother kept an eye on the tables in Homburg, a heavily capitalized Belgian *contrebanque*, or gambling syndicate, playing trente-et-quarante according to a so-called infallible system, laid a determined siege to the bank. Thackeray, under the pseudonym of Mr M. A. Titmarsh, described the episode in a little-known novel, *The Kickleburys on the Rhine*; Homburg is 'Rougetnoirburg' and François Blanc is 'Monsieur Lenoir':

> When the Contrebanque arrived . . . all the minor punters, and gamblers, ceased their peddling play, and looked on in silence round the verdant plain, where the greatest combat was to be decided. Not used to the vast operations of war, like his brother, Lenoir Junior telegraphed to his absent chief the news of the mighty enemy who had come down upon him, asked for instructions, and in the meanwhile met the foeman like a man. The Contrebanque gallantly opened its campaign.
>
> The Lenoir bank was defeated day after day, in numerous encounters. The tactics of the Contrebanquist generals were irresistible: their infernal system bore down everything before it, and they marched onwards terrible, and victorious, as the Macedonian Phalanx . . . Rouleau after rouleau* fell into their possession. At last the news came: the Emperor had joined the Grand Army. Lenoir himself had arrived from Paris, and was once more among his children, his people. The daily combats

* Since counters had not yet been adopted at this time, real coins or banknotes were staked, large sums being wrapped up in *rouleaux*, or rolls of stiff paper, on which was printed their value.

continued . . . With a devilish forbearance and coolness, the atrocious Contrebanque, like Polyphemus, who only took one of his prisoners out of the cave at a time, and so ate them off at leisure, the horrid Contrebanquists, I say, contented themselves with winning so much before dinner, and so much before supper – say five thousand florins for each meal. They played and won at noon: they played and won at eventide . . . What must have been the feelings of the great Lenoir? What were those of Washington, before Trenton? . . .

At last there came one day when the Contrebanquists had won their allotted sum, and were about to leave the tables which they had swept so often. But pride, and lust of gold had seized upon the heart of one of their vainglorious chieftains; and he said, 'Do not let us go yet – let us win a thousand florins more!'

Some three hours afterwards – a shout, a mighty shout was heard around the windows of the palace: the town, the gardens, the hills, the fountains took up and echoed the jubilant acclaim. Hip, Hip, Hip, Hurrah, Hurrah, Hurrah! People rushed into each other's arms, men, women, and children cried, and kissed each other. Croupiers, who never feel, who never tremble, who never care whether black wins, or red loses, took snuff from each other's boxes, and laughed for joy; and Lenoir, the dauntless, the INVINCIBLE, Lenoir, wiped the drops of perspiration from his calm forehead, as he drew the enemy's last rouleau into his till. He had conquered . . .

'He who breaks the bank today will assuredly return to be broken by the bank tomorrow.' François Blanc's dictum had been proved and the crisis had left his nerve intact. He pursued his policy of lavish outlay and made further plans for an expansion that would keep step with the ever-increasing swarm of visitors.

Living in a small villa opposite the casino with an old housekeeper as his only servant, he spent little on himself. His mistress was dead, his brother was ill enough to have been moved to a nursing home where he eventually died, and his two small sons were away at boarding school. True Frenchman that he was, he had never felt at home in Germany and he missed the company of his fellow-countrymen. There were plenty of visiting Frenchmen, but they were hardly likely to make a friend of a man who was enriching himself at their expense. He was very lonely, and all the more delighted when his servant brought a lovely sixteen-year-old girl called Marie Hensel to help her with the housework. Chiefly, perhaps, because she spoke French, she made an immediate impression on him. She came from a nearby village called Fried-richsdorf which had been founded in 1685 by Huguenot refugees whose descendants still stuck to their mother-tongue, and this asset, with her beauty and vivacity, set him thinking seriously of marriage. Lack of refinement and knowledge of the world were the only drawback; she might have embarrassed him in the fashionable circles he had to move in. He decided to correct her education by sending her to school in France. By the time she came of age, he hoped, she would pass muster as a woman of the world. Until then, as Charles Graves aptly puts it, the Almanach de Gotha was to be her bedside book.

Homburg meanwhile – 'the rendez-vous of travellers', as the advertisements proclaimed, 'the elegant and fashionable retreat of people of taste, leisure and wit, and a peaceful oasis visited yearly by whole caravans of tourists who may well be called the pilgrims of pleasure' – continued to prosper. Among these pilgrims was Napoleon's nephew, Prince Charles Lucien Bonaparte. He arrived in Homburg in September 1852, and the directors of the casino were delighted to welcome such a distinguished visitor. His violent passion for gambling was proverbial: he was said to shrink from nothing but small stakes. Their delight began to fade when he won ninety thousand gulden in four days; if his luck continued, he would exhaust the bank's entire reserves. Fortunately, during a forty-eight hours' absence from the tables, other players lost enough to make up for his winnings; but the evening he returned, in spite of losing heavily until ten o'clock, he ended up with a further 280,000 gulden, and left Homburg next morning with his winnings intact.

His departure may have been prompted by the directors' desperate decision to reduce the maximum stake from four to two thousand gulden. Such was their panic, they even considered introducing the *double refait* at trente-et-quarante and a second zero at roulette. All this ran counter to François Blanc's policy of 'throwing sprats to catch whales', as he put it, 'and trusting to goddess Fortune'. He had been absent when the prince arrived. Calm as ever, he hailed Bonaparte's run of luck as a splendid advertisement for the casino, and he was right. There was a spectacular rise in the number of visitors, the losses were soon retrieved, and by the following year profits were higher than ever.

His personal affairs were also taking a cheerful turn. Marie had made such good progress at her finishing school that he was determined to bring her back to Homburg as his wife. The marriage, which took place on 20 June 1854, was as successful as any of his other speculations; the former servant girl turned out to be a shrewd and efficient business partner as well as a devoted and decorative consort. In three years she learnt enough of the running of the casino to take the place of Louis and to deputize for her husband when he was away.

As business continued to boom, Blanc felt he could now afford to choose his clients more carefully. His initial *Règlements du Service des Salles de Jeu* provided for the supervision of the croupiers and the casino staff, but there was still no check on the gamblers themselves. At least half of them were arrant rascals, according to a contemporary eye-witness, 'rascals male and rascals female, *chevaliers d'industrie*, the sweepings of all the gambling-houses in Europe, *lorettes*, and demireps and the like . . .' Shady characters, including Countess Kisselev's 'professors', still haunted the tables and one day a Frenchman was caught red-handed playing with a sham *rouleau* of coins of which only the two end pieces were gold; the rest were lead. Blanc decided to extend his surveillance system to the players. *Livres de jeu* were instituted, in which the names of visitors were amplified by some characteristic of their dress or appearance – 'the Englishman with spectacles', 'the new client with fair whiskers', 'the Russian with the wooden leg', and so on. By these means anyone who had proved undesirable could be spotted and refused admittance. Dostoevsky's eye-witness description of the casino about this time shows how badly these measures were needed:

At the roulette tables and at the other end of the room, at the table for trente-et-quarante, there was a crowd of a hundred and fifty or two hundred players, several rows deep. Those who had managed to squeeze their way up to the table held fast as they always do, refusing to give up their places to anyone until they had lost; simple spectators were not allowed to stand at the tables and occupy the space. Though there were chairs round the table, few of the players sat down, especially when there was a great crowd, because one could get closer standing and pick one's place and place one's stake more conveniently. The second and the third rows pressed on the first, waiting and watching for their turn; but sometimes a hand would reach impatiently through the first row and put down a coin. Even from the third row people managed to seize chances of poking their stakes forward; consequently every five minutes there was some 'scene' over disputed stakes at one end of the hall or another. But the police of the casino were fairly good. It was impossible to prevent crowding: in fact the owners were glad of the crush of people because of the profits, but eight croupiers sitting round the table kept vigilant watch; they even kept count of the stakes, and when disputes arose, they settled them.

By 1857 the company's financial position was strong enough for Blanc to increase the bank's reserves from four hundred thousand to six hundred thousand gulden, and profits continued to increase during the next three years. Plans were made and fresh capital was raised for the construction of new buildings in view of the opening of the Homburg–Frankfurt railway. This was expected to take place on 10 September 1860, but in a single month the exploits of a gambler even more intrepid and successful than Prince Lucien Bonaparte threatened all those projects with failure.

Tomás García was the son of a rich Barcelona landowner. Sent to Paris at the age of twenty-three to represent a Spanish cork company, he took to gambling and was so lucky that by 1860 he had made enough to try out his talents at Homburg. It was said, however, that his good fortune was not all luck; there were rumours of loaded dice and marked cards. His appearance was not prepossessing. His features were undistinguished; he was short and stocky, and there was something of the sailor in his gait. He made up for his plebeian looks by flashy clothes and flashier jewellery. He was accompanied by a beautiful German mistress and a man whom he passed off as his brother, and these two retainers added to his aura of ostentation. They also served as accomplices; the maximum individual stake at Homburg was now fixed at six thousand gulden and the total stakes at any one table were limited to thirty thousand on a single coup. By staking simultaneously they were thus able to complete the table's maximum between them.

This they proceeded to do. They started on 24 August, a Friday. During the day they won 14,000 gulden and 84,500 on Saturday and on Sunday, 55,000. They lost the whole of the previous days' winnings on Monday but on Tuesday they got 130,000 gulden back in less than an hour. They lost 22,000 later in the day, but on Wednesday they scored again to the tune of 120,000, ending up with a total profit of over 200,000 gulden.

By now García was a local celebrity. A contemporary observer records:

> Crowds of people stand outside the doors of the kursaal every morning, and when he stops playing they accompany him to the door in a shower of congratulations ... See how they make way for him at the tables, how deferential their subdued greetings! Banking on his luck, he does not bring much money with him. When the croupiers see him place a stake on the table, they at once get ready to pay him out without waiting to see if he has actually won. It is even rumoured that they have offered him a handsome sum down to desist from playing ...

True or not, he and his accomplices and his winnings vanished from Homburg for ten days. But they were back again on 9 September, when they promptly won a further 122,000 gulden. They suffered their greatest reverse next day, losing 228,500 in six hours, but they got them back in the next forty-eight hours. 'It can no longer be called play,' the government commissioner gravely reported to the landgrave:

García sweeps the board the moment he arrives and all day long fresh sums have to be poured into the bank; then the bank impoverishes him to such an extent that he has to send to France for cash. It's the same wretched business day after day. The watching crowd is indescribable and so dense that it is impossible to keep order. But the moral effect is even worse. Homburg is already under attack – 'a den of thieves', and so on – and its reputation is bound to suffer. If the doings are repeated, the papers will have plenty to say.

When the García syndicate left two days later, they had won nearly half a million gulden and wiped out the bank's entire profits for the whole season; and the papers were full of it. Only Blanc retained his wonted calm; he knew full well that the publicity surrounding so sensational a series of winnings would put everything right in the end, and he was sure that García, unlike Prince Lucien Bonaparte, would be back. He was right on both counts: García was in Homburg again in October 1861 and within twenty-four hours he lost 22,000 gulden – at that time all he possessed. Countless other players had sought to emulate his earlier exploit and none had succeeded. Among them was George Augustus Sala, a *Daily Telegraph* correspondent at that time. He described himself as the Man with the Iron Chest, referring to the coffer for the fortune he planned to win at Homburg. He had a wonderful system, and before leaving from England he had tried it out successfully with what he called 'blank cartridges', using beans in lieu of coins. But once in Homburg, he complained that the blaze of the chandeliers and the clinking of the money somehow got into his head and threw everything into confusion. He ended with a rueful warning: 'Be wise ere you steam up the Rhine towards Homburg-von-der-Höhe; for if you go there, and be made of ordinary flesh and blood – I am not writing for oysters or icebergs – you must play, and will in all human possibility leave your skin behind you.'

Most people did, and in 1852 the profits rose to nearly a million and a half gulden. Those of Monaco had sunk to a mere sixty thousand francs.

5

MONACO
TRANSFORMED

Blanc had been keeping a watchful eye on Monaco for years. Ever since the Société des Bains de Mer was founded, he had been sending emissaries posing as ordinary members of the public, and after the failure of the original concessionaires he had been able to follow developments more closely still, for several of the croupiers had deserted and he had promptly dispatched some of his own Homburg staff to fill the vacancies and keep him regularly informed. He knew every detail of Lefebvre's mismanagement and all the problems of the Duc de Valmy and his associates.

He had long toyed with the idea of the Monaco concession. Now, if ever, was the moment to capture it. He was experienced enough; he was certainly rich enough – his fortune was reckoned to be twenty million francs at least – and his reputation was intact. What is more, he was growing dissatisfied at Homburg. He hated the Germanic atmosphere and longed for a more congenial one. Since the García crisis his colleagues had become increasingly ill-disposed: they criticized his policy and blamed him for the slightest setback. The shareholders too had begun to intrigue against him. While he was away in Switzerland taking the cure at Loèche-les-Bains, they induced the landgrave's government to pass a law restricting the powers of the concessionaire. It was a surly trick. Blanc alone had turned this little mid-German town into a city of palaces, the prosperity of the inhabitants was entirely his work. He was genuinely hurt by the hostility and ingratitude behind it, and all the more ready therefore to move to a place where lack of government short-sightedness and interference might give his talents free play.

Blanc, now fifty-seven, was energetically supported by his wife. She had persistently warned that German gambling was bound to be abolished one day, and in the Prussian Upper House this threat was becoming audible as well as in the Federal Diet of Frankfurt. She had the perspicacity to see that the unification of Germany and the doom of small principalities like Hesse-Homburg was on the way. Her husband assured her that the landgrave had given him every guarantee: she would retort by asking who had guaranteed the landgrave. She too felt ill at ease in the little spa; her humble origins were known to all; she longed to start afresh where her self-assurance, social grace and her privileged position might be given a better chance.

In spite of his ardour for fresh fields, François Blanc was too astute, however, to make the first move himself: he could afford to wait for an overture from the Duc de Valmy. Meanwhile, through a man called Bigy, the former director of the Cercle Saint-Hubert in Paris and a close friend of Lefebvre, discreet hints were dropped in Monaco that he might not be deaf to suggestions. The bait was eagerly seized and before long he was invited to Paris for discussions with Valmy and Eynaud. He remained standing during the interview and declared himself to be suffering from an inconveniently located boil; and the ailment – which may have been genuine, for he was subject to skin infections – gave him a pretext for postponing negotiations until he could embark on a proper session. Before committing himself any further, he wrote to Prince Charles and suggested forming a company with a capital of twelve million francs. The funds were to be laid out in buildings similar to the Homburg casino and in providing amenities which would make Monaco secure against all competition from Nice. 'If these plans are to be carried out,' he added, 'the concession should be made available for a reasonable sum.'

At this stage Valmy and Lefebvre made a mistake. They demanded 1,860,000 francs. This was not really an enormous sum for the man who had made a fortune out of Homburg – as Eynaud pointed out to the prince, a hundred thousand francs were no more to Blanc than a hundred to other people – but Blanc was shrewd enough to see that he could bring down the price. He broke off negotiations and put his reasons before the prince by letter:

> For reasons which it is not for me to particularize the management of these gentlemen is driving the business from bad to worse. They now base their proposals upon the enhanced value which would accrue as the result of my experience and capital: M. Lefebvre's approach to me is telling proof of their embarrassment. In the hands of an enlightened and well organized company, Monaco could become one of the most popular winter resorts in the Mediterranean. I request Your Serene Highness to intervene and reduce their demands to a reasonable figure.

But Valmy and Lefebvre stubbornly refused to bring down the price until an unexpected event made them change their minds.

The new casino on the Spélugues – 'a vast and magnificent establishment', according to the local press – had at last been opened. In fact it was a poky and jerry-built affair. Only three of its rooms – the ballroom, the concert room and the gaming room, the last of which was also used as a reading and smoking room – were furnished, and the bare walls and bad lighting gave them a gloomy and almost funereal aspect. Nevertheless crowds of curious sightseers flocked to the opening and some of them stayed to play. Among them was Tomás García. It has been suggested that Blanc himself had secretly encouraged the presence of the intrepid and successful gambler at this particular moment. His fame was such that his very appearance at the trente-et-quarante table was enough to set the management trembling, and when he proceeded to clean up forty-five thousand francs Valmy and Lefebvre hurriedly reopened negotiations in a more conciliatory spirit.

Blanc offered 1,129,000 francs, a larger sum than anyone had expected; yet Valmy and Lefebvre continued to quibble over details, refusing to clinch the deal until they had had further discussions. Determined to put an end to this temporizing, Blanc announced his impending arrival. He reached Monaco by the morning boat from Nice and drove straight to the casino. 'These,' he said to the director, holding them up, 'are three bonds on the

Bank of France. They are worth 1,100,000 francs. You wish to sell the concession and I am prepared to buy it. I am lunching at Monaco. The *Palmaria* sails at four o'clock and I want the matter settled before I leave.'

It worked. An agreement was signed, and on 1 April the Société des Bains de Mer et Cercle des Etrangers was founded with a capital of eight million francs. The sum was divided into 32,000 shares of 250 francs each, of which Blanc received 18,800, and 4,000 were taken up by his secretary – a man called Desportes – and by a friend of his wife's called Antoine Bertora. The remaining 9,200 were to be issued at a slower pace and against full payment. The bishop of Monaco was one of the earliest shareholders. Another was Cardinal Pecci, later elected Pope as Leo xiii. The concession was to last fifty years. For the first ten of them Blanc was appointed to be the general managing director. He was to pay the prince an annually increasing sum proportionate to the profits and share some of the expense of completing the coast road from Nice, which only went as far as Villefranche.

The takeover was enthusiastically hailed by the inhabitants. 'An entire and brilliant transformation,' was Eynaud's prediction. 'The new management will do great things,' the press announced, 'and in the grand style. M. Blanc's name and reputation are a sure guarantee.' His mere presence, in fact, had already caused a fantastic rise in the price of Spélugues and Condamine building-sites. The bank itself enjoyed a period of unwonted prosperity. García won 70,000 francs and lost them all again, together with another 20,000, and had to borrow his fare home from the casino.

Blanc's first move was to increase the reserves at the trente-et-quarante tables to a hundred thousand francs and those at roulette to half that amount. Jacobi, his Homburg architect, condemned the casino building out of hand. Blanc fitted out the existing gaming rooms as luxuriously as possible until the new plans for its enlargement and embellishment could be carried out. He urged on the construction of the Hôtel de Paris. He wanted it to be unique in luxury and comfort and to surpass all the greatest hotels in the world – even magnificent places like the Hôtel du Louvre and the

Grand Hôtel in Paris – in its decoration, its furniture, its equipment and its cuisine. Most importantly, he inspired the inhabitants
with a sense of purpose. Dreaming inaction, he proclaimed, must
give way to courage and activity. 'There is a whole town to be
built! To work, then!' He set the example by buying a stretch of
land near the Sainte-Dévote ravine and building himself a pretty
villa there. Other building-sites were offered at very low prices.
Thanks to his name they were eagerly snapped up and, although
the roads were still bad, the number of visitors to the casino in 1863
rose to 27,872 – twice as many as in 1861. The profits for the year
were six hundred and forty thousand francs – a very small increase
on the previous year and far from commensurate with the vast
outlay – but Blanc was confident that it would be recovered as soon
as the railway line reached Monaco. By now it had got as far as
Cagnes.

By the start of 1864, things were getting ahead. The old
Palmaria had been joined by the new *Solferino*, and there was a
regular bus service to Nice. The Hôtel de Paris was still unfinished,
but the restaurant had been in action since New Year's Eve, and its
splendour augured well for the rest of the building. Two hundred
thousand francs had been spent on the table silver alone. The
gaming rooms were put under the management of a brother-in-law
of Marie Blanc's called Henri Wagatha. They were as carefully run
as those at Homburg and were doing so well that Blanc decided to
do away with the second zero at roulette. In July the Hôtel de Paris
was opened; it was furnished, someone said, with the taste of an
intelligent millionaire. The bathing establishment in the Condamine, managed by Dr Gillebert d'Herbourt, was opened in
November. M. André, meanwhile, the designer of the Parc
Monceau, was laying out the casino gardens. New Year's Day of
1865 was marked by the opening of the Salle Mauresque. Designed
by M. Dutrou, the architect of the Palais de l'Industrie, it was the
first addition to the casino building. Large enough to hold five
tables for roulette or trente-et-quarante, it was thought to be very
original and exotic.*

---

* All trace of Moorish art has now disappeared. Subsequently known as the
Salle Schmidt, it was renovated in 1968 and rechristened the Salle de l'Europe.

Publicity was one of Blanc's main preoccupations during this period. He had virtual control over the local press, and in Paris he relied on the services of Henri de Villemessant, unscrupulous founder-editor of the influential and scandal-mongering *Figaro*. He had already dealt with him in Homburg days and knew that he could be suborned. He sold him one of the best sites in the Condamine for much less than it was worth and invited him down to his own villa; lavish hospitality and flattery were rewarded by fulsome articles extolling Monaco as a spa and an investment:

> Here is where I would gladly pitch my tent. Two or three million francs' worth of land will be worth four times as much in two or three years' time. M. Blanc has transformed a region which was once pleasing rather than rich into a veritable California. He does not discover gold mines, he creates them. M. Blanc is a bold but sagacious gambler, both self-controlled and accurate in his calculations. He has both vision and judgement. It is as though Monaco had been touched by a fairy's magic wand . . . In eighteen months' time, when one will be able to make the journey in fifteen minutes by train, Monaco will be the Bois de Boulogne of Nice . . .

Blanc himself reckoned that the line would be ready by 1867 or 1868. He had less than three years in which to build a model town for the flood of expected visitors, and most of the company's increasing profits were swallowed up in the outlay. Wagatha was deeply concerned. The bank had suffered a number of severe reverses. At a single session two players from Lyons had carried off a hundred and fifty thousand francs, almost a third of the total reserves. But Blanc, as usual, remained as calm and confident as ever. By the beginning of 1866 his confidence was shown to be justified. The fame of Monaco had crossed the seas and visitors now included such distinguished gamblers as the Duke of Hamilton, Lord Stafford, Princess Souvaroff and the indefatigable Countess Kisselev. They also included the poet and historian of the Renaissance, John Addington Symonds. His diary entry for 22 March is a long and luxuriant paean about the casino – 'the large house of sin, blazing with gas lamps by night . . . flaming and shining by the shore like Pandemonium, or the habitation of some romantic witch. The place, in truth, resembles the gardens of Alcina or any other magician's trap for catching souls, which poets have devised . . .' He went on to describe the gaming rooms themselves:

> Play was going forward like a business. Roulette and rouge-et-noir tables were crowded. Little could be heard but the monotonous voice of the croupiers, the rattle of gold under the wooden shovels, and the clinking of the ball that spun round for roulette. Imperturbable gravity sat on the faces of the men who lost or won. Several stern-faced women were making small stakes, and accurately pricking all the chances of the game on cards . . .

About the casino staff, he remarked:

> The croupiers are either fat, sensual cormorants or sallow, lean-cheeked vultures, or suspicious foxes. So I term them; yet they only look like wicked bankers' clerks, like men narrowed and made void by constant contact with money in a heartless trade, and corrupted by familiarity with turns of luck instead of honourable business rules. Compare them with Coutts' men to note the difference. It is very discernible, for, though in externals much alike, these men of the gaming bank show every trace of a dissolute youth and a vile calling, of low sensuality and hardened avarice, upon their faces . . .

Almost all the gamblers, he said, had light blue eyes . . . His strictures are an echo of Balzac's opening pages in *La Peau de Chagrin*; they were to be re-echoed again and again by later critics.

A regular campaign against the casino was being promoted in some of the other coast towns, and ruin at the tables was their war cry. Meetings of protest were held in the streets of Nice. Léon Pilatte, a pastor of the Reformed Church, went so far as to publish a remonstrance against Prince Charles himself. Hostile articles appeared in the local newspapers and especially in the *Journal des Etrangers*. A petition was signed by the leading inhabitants demanding the immediate suspension of the casino, and travellers arriving at Nice by train – the railway line had reached Nice by now – were warned against the wicked seductions of Monaco by a series of placards like Hogarth caricatures. Bribery – Blanc's usual method of silencing such attacks – failed to take effect. He decided to ignore them, trusting that the outcry would subside of its own accord. The usual solution, far from silencing the enemy, seemed to transform it into a hydra. Meanwhile, he proposed a system of entrance cards. The public was notified that henceforth 'clerks, domestic servants, labourers and peasants' would not be admitted. The system excluded the lower strata of the population but, much more importantly, malicious journalists and other undesirables, and one of the first to be refused a card was the proprietor of the *Journal des Etrangers*.

By now the principality had expanded into three distinct areas. The Rock, as the prince's residence and the seat of government, remained relatively unchanged, but the old Condamine gardens were becoming a commercial centre, and the houses and villas on the barren promontory round the casino were turning it into a residential area. A separate name was clearly needed for this model town. It might have been called Les Spélugues, but although the word, in its older French form, meant nothing worse than a cave, it had unpleasant connotations in Italian and German. Alternative styles – Charlesville or Albertville, to be named after the prince or his son – had been suggested when the foundation stone of the casino was laid; but they thought it best to keep the sovereign's name clear of such dubious concerns. Blanc felt that the time had now come to adorn the new city with a name that would be worthy of its future and he accordingly approached the prince.

Charles III had no qualms about lending his name to so promising a project: so, on 1 July 1866, a fiat went forth: everything east of the Sainte-Dévote ravine was henceforth to be known as Monte Carlo. Within a few months the new syllables were to eclipse the name of the principality itself.

6

FROM STRENGTH TO STRENGTH

With Monte Carlo, Blanc's reputation was, quite literally, based on rock. Lord Brougham, who drove over to call on him from Cannes, thought him one of the foremost and most capable financiers of France: 'He astonished me again and again by his simplicity and at the same time by the range of his foresight.' These opinions were echoed by Sir Charles Dilke, who compared him favourably 'in tact, in conversational force and in the way he united decisiveness and an open mind' with Adolphe Thiers, the elder statesman and historian.

He was now sixty but, with his high complexion, thin and greasy hair and the wispy moustache which shaded a rather forbidding and thin-lipped mouth, he looked older. Gold-rimmed spectacles – less to correct faulty vision than to mask the darting and deep-set eyes behind them, for these instruments of intimidation never looked through them but always over the top – were perched on the end of a long and probing nose. Short and slight in build, he was very sensitive to the cold and was always enveloped in a heavy grey overcoat. With shoulders hunched and leaning on a gold-handled cane, he dragged his feet as though the trouser straps under the insteps prevented him from lifting them, and he was so absorbed in his own thoughts that he rarely raised his glance from the ground to return a greeting.

His friends and acquaintances were equally scarce; his unsociability tended to keep strangers at a distance. This aloofness was also prompted by a secret fear: perhaps some adventurer might kill him for his money . . . With this is mind, he kept only small sums of cash in his pocket and this caution, sometimes misinterpreted as stinginess, set him at a still further remove. Lavishness was inevitably expected from someone in his position but, for all his wealth, he could not afford it. Every risk was carefully pondered, and rightly, for his present heavy expenses had no hope of being recovered for years. Luckily there was a steady profit from Homburg, but this was not likely to last much longer. Like Monte Carlo, Homburg had become a target for criticism. A play had recently come out in Frankfurt called *Rien ne va plus!* It was set in 'Hontebourg-sur-l'Abîme' and 'Monsieur Noir', manager of 'the world's premier gambling-hell at Shameville-in-the Pit', was a transparent portrait of himself.

It was merely a question of time before gambling was abolished in the landgrave's territory. During the Seven Weeks' War of 1866 Hesse-Homburg had sided with Austria in her struggle with Prussia over the hegemony of the German Confederation. Blanc's confident hopes of an Austrian victory – shared by most Frenchmen – were shattered on the field of Königsgrätz. The peace treaty incorporated Homburg in Prussia, and Prussia had been opposed to all gambling within its former frontiers. The little town was spared for the time being however, and its fame was even enhanced when Dostoevsky's *Gambler* came out.

Drawn there by tales of fabulous winnings, Dostoevsky had first visited the Rhineland in 1862 and four days at the roulette tables of Wiesbaden had been his undoing. Beginner's luck – 'I won, not as much as I could have wished, but still a nice little sum' – had led him to suppose that he had discovered the secret of gambling. 'It is extremely stupid and extremely simple: constant self-control, imperturbable, come what may. That is all. With this rule of conduct it is impossible to lose.' He discovered his error during his first visit to Homburg in October 1863, but he came back regularly during the next ten years and always lost. By 1867 he was utterly disenchanted with the place but could not tear himself away. 'Yesterday was a horrible day,' he wrote to his wife. 'I played for ten hours, and lost. I am making my last attempt today.' At the end of it he was forced to pawn his watch. A week later he gave up gambling for good: 'I want to come home. Send me twenty imperials at once.' Three days after getting them he wrote that he had lost them all . . . 'down to the last kreutzer'. This time his wife came all the way from St Petersburg and fetched him back herself.

He gambled for such small sums that his name was not even entered on the Homburg registers, unlike the Russian chancellor Gortchakoff, who laid down his stakes in thousands, or the Turkish general called Mustapha Fazil Pasha, who lost more than 150,000 gulden at trente-et-quarante in the space of ten minutes. Thanks to people like these, the Homburg bank made a profit of over a million gulden a year; but on 28 February 1868 the dreaded law was passed by the Prussian chamber; it was to come into force on 1 January 1873, after which Blanc would have to rely on Monte Carlo alone.

The appearance of the principality had been transformed beyond recognition. The harbour and jetty of the Condamine were finished, and a water supply and lighting system had been installed. Charming fenced residences embedded in greenery were spaced out along the broad and gas-lit boulevards. The bathing establishment, served by an hotel, specialized in carbonic-acid baths, massage, showers, Zander gymnastics and electric and X-ray treatment. Sea-bathing was becoming so popular that instructions had to be issued regarding life-saving and diet. The *Journal de Monaco* advised all bathers to adopt the English custom of a large breakfast starting with watercress. A paved roadway ascended from the Condamine to Monte Carlo, where villas were springing up on all sides. A large café had opened near the casino and a second hotel was under construction. The Hôtel de Paris, under the personal supervision of Marie Blanc, was already famous. A first-class dinner cost five francs, and even this small charge was waived if the client were a *décavé* who had lost all his money at the tables.

The coast road was incomplete and most visitors still came by sea, but the old *Palmaria* had now been replaced by the *Charles III*, a 120-ft, 60-horsepower and much faster vessel which Blanc had had built at his own expense at Bordeaux. The railway line was slowly advancing. Dwarfing the little chapel of Sainte-Dévote, the viaduct which was to carry the track across the ravine was already built, and all that remained to be built was the last of the tunnels; these had had to be cut through the solid rock at eleven points along the seashore. Blanc had insisted on a station at Monte Carlo in addition to the original one planned for Monaco, and had bought the land out of his own pocket and offered it free to the railway company. The approach of the railway led to vast speculation in land. The Bellevue property for which Langlois and Aubert had paid 64,000 francs was divided into lots sold for 1,500,000 francs each. A smaller piece of land in the Condamine, which the former owner had cheerfully sold for 1,200 francs and a handful of cigars, now fetched 70,000 francs.

Towards the end of September the *Journal de Monaco* reported that the blond whiskers of the first Englishman of the season had been spotted in the casino gardens. He was the harbinger of a winter influx which turned out larger than ever; for at last, on 19 October, the railway reached Monaco. The bank's profits for 1868–9 rose to 2,386,000 francs and the principality itself had become so prosperous that on 8 February the prince issued a decree that did away with all direct taxation of his subjects. The chief cause of their previous discontent had now vanished.

Monte Carlo, in the *franglais* of the time, was '*le rendez-vous de la fashion européenne*'. It far eclipsed even Baden-Baden in elegance and distinction. To attract the aristocracy of the gambling world as well as high society, Blanc put up the maximum stake to twelve thousand francs. It was a direct challenge to the rich and dashing players, like Princess Souvaroff, and on 17 April she launched a well-planned onslaught on the bank. She started by losing three hundred thousand francs and ended the day by carrying off seven hundred thousand and went on winning for nearly a month. But her luck abandoned her at last and all her winnings found their way back to source. Other gamblers had better luck. Six players once carried off nearly a million francs and sometimes the bank's losses were so heavy, particularly at trente-et-quarante, that the company's capital was in serious danger. These crises were always transitory, for however great an individual win, sooner or later it was inevitably made up for by the overall losses of the general public. But Blanc's fellow-directors were haunted all that year by the nightmare of another García or Bonaparte descending upon them.

But when García reappeared in 1869 he was no longer the flamboyant figure who had terrorized Homburg and set Valmy and Lefebvre shaking like aspen-leaves. Shortly after his previous visit he had been caught with marked cards at a private baccara party and sentenced to five years' imprisonment. In view of this, Blanc felt justified in refusing him admittance. He left the principality forever, a seedy old jailbird now, to be swallowed up in the Paris underworld. He died in want about ten years later.

The fortunes of the casino were soaring. Besides the railway from Nice, Blanc had persuaded the Paris-Lyons-Marseilles company to run a first-class express from Cannes, which reached Monte Carlo at noon and returned in time for the passengers to be home for dinner; and by the end of 1869 the number of visitors broke all records. The profits of the bank were correspondingly larger but they were not enough to cover the vast outlay. For the time being, only the prince and his subjects derived any tangible benefit from the casino. Yet even though Blanc's enterprise had exempted them from direct taxation, the Monégasques felt little gratitude. Monte Carlo, they considered, and with some justification, was being developed at Monaco's expense: the old town enjoyed none of the amenities provided for the new resort, and they were indignant that the company employed no local contractors.

Blanc's nominee as foreman of works was a sinister figure named Doineau, said to have robbed a diligence in Algeria while working for the military government. A passenger had been killed during the hold-up and Doineau had been condemned to death. He was later reprieved by Napoleon III on condition that he left French territory, and had come to Monaco where his energy and powers of organization had quickly endeared him to Blanc. But his slave-driving methods were hated by the Monégasque labourers, and their complaints became so loud and bitter that early in 1870 he dismissed them all and replaced them with Piedmontese workmen. Meetings of protest were organized while Blanc was away in Paris and a procession marched up the palace with a petition to the prince outlining his subjects' grievances. Above all, they demanded Doineau's expulsion from the principality. It was the feast of Sainte-Dévote, and the National Guard, on parade for the celebrations, started fraternizing with the demonstrators and joining in their demands.

The temper was such that the prince had no alternative but to agree. Yet, even after Doineau had been escorted to the station and put on board a train by the police, the population was still hostile enough for the governor-general of the principality to recommend closing down the casino. Eynaud was so perturbed that he advised the prince to disband the National Guard. But the prince was so blind – not only, it seemed, from his physical affliction but also with rage – that he threatened to withdraw Blanc's concession. In the end a middle course was found. The National Guard was disbanded and reorganized on more practical lines. Blanc no longer insisted on Doineau's recall and agreed to provide the old town with the improvements which the Monégasques demanded.

His relations with the prince were improved, but there were other matters which caused him anxiety. Threats were now a part of the press campaign against the casino and hardly a day passed without anonymous letters threatening him and his fellow-directors with violence or death. A pair of blackmailers from Nice even broke into his wife's apartments. All these things imposed a severe strain on his nerves and, with increasing age and deteriorating health, he began to lose some of his former energy. He could no longer overlook the hostility of the local newspapers, yet he now felt unequal to fighting them on their own ground. To conciliate and silence them, he filled them with advertisements. Once begun, the expense was a permanent and substantial drain.

The outbreak of the Franco-Prussian War on 19 July 1870 put Blanc in a difficult position. He was a loyal Frenchman, all of his sympathies lay with France; besides, he hated Bismarck's government, which was responsible for the impending doom at Homburg. But all his wife's relations were German – three of her brothers were serving under the Prussian flag – and so were most of his staff, and the press was quick to suspect them as spies. He forbade all his German employees to leave the principality for the duration of the war and when, after a series of French defeats, his German gardener was heard to shout 'Long live Prussia! Down with France!' he promptly dismissed him. But – especially when the casino at Homburg was forced to subscribe a large sum to the Prussian war loan – the hostile press campaign continued; all he could do was present an equally large sum to the French. Denied access to Germany, he arranged for his architect Jacobi to keep the Homburg casino open. It was a wise course: his Russian clients – who were by far the most profitable – were as bent on gambling as ever and, even though the number of visitors and the takings dropped, the casino still prospered.

Business at Monte Carlo steadily declined. As the news from the front grew more depressing the number of visitors fell off; play continued, but half-heartedly, and for the first time since Blanc had taken over the profits failed to cover the expenses. The political situation was getting worse. Rumours began to predict the dethronement of Napoleon III and the proclamation of a republic. Blanc had fears of a revolutionary movement in Nice and armed bands attacking Monaco. The thought so alarmed him that he asked permission to close the casino for a time, though he knew it would prevent him from covering his daily overheads. 'Monsieur Blanc may be precipitate,' the government commissioner reported, 'but the Prussians are advancing fast and the Empire faces a dire situation. The casino is still deserted.'

The emperor surrendered at Sedan, a republic was proclaimed two days later, and Blanc's alarm turned to panic. Haunted by the thought of an onslaught from Nice, he hired a gang of workmen – supposedly to lay out some new gardens but really to protect the casino – and four days later he persuaded the prince to let him suspend play.

He had strong grounds for misgivings; things were unfolding just as he had foreseen. In three weeks Paris was under German siege and the populace, enraged by the inaction of the provisional government, was loud in protest. At the end of October a commune was declared in Paris, and soon red flags were fluttering in Lyons and in the provinces. Disorder and rioting spread to Marseilles and threatened Nice. Goaded by the tension, Blanc called on the prefect of the Alpes Maritimes: what measures were being taken in the event of a popular uprising? For the first time since the outbreak of the war he received some comfort. The prefect told him there was no danger of the régime being overthrown. But business in Nice was at a standstill. The closing of the Monte Carlo casino had reduced the stream of visitors to a trickle and the local tradespeople longed for gambling to start again. Even Blanc's noisiest opponents were now begging for it, and this unexpected turn gave him a handy argument against future traducers. So, with confidence restored, he decided to reopen on 1 December.

Another chance of winning favour with the population and at the same time of displaying his patriotism was soon to crop up. When Nice failed to raise the great sum demanded by the national defence loan, he personally subscribed the balance; and when peace was declared and Prussia imposed a two hundred million francs indemnity on her victim, he gave two million francs of his own fortune to the French government. He could afford to do so. In spite of the closing of the casino, the company had declared a dividend of 5 per cent for 1870 and at Homburg business had been even better. He now felt so sure of himself that when the Nice press resumed their attacks he took the offensive and won a libel action against the *Réveil des Alpes Maritimes*.

Pessimists might declare that Monte Carlo was doomed – the French government was trying to persuade Prince Charles to cancel the concession, and it was even rumoured that the principality might be annexed by the new republic – but Blanc went ahead with all the schemes he had had to shelve during the fighting. As long ago as 1854 he had thought of pigeon-shooting competitions in Homburg as an extra draw, but he had been dissuaded on the grounds that the proximity of firearms might encourage suicide. But he had stuck to the idea and new plans were made for Monte Carlo. The tip of the promontory below the casino was chosen and a semicircular terrace was hoisted on a series of arches springing from the rough rocks and the shore. Plans were also made to enlarge the casino itself and make room for the large crowds which Blanc hoped that peacetime would bring. He was right yet again: by the end of the year the swarm of visitors reached an unprecedented total.

Thus 1872 began with glowing prospects. In February the *tir aux pigeons* opened with a competition and a first prize of two thousand francs. Four hundred of them were spent by the American winner – his name was George Lorillard – on a cable to New York announcing his victory. It was a bumper success. The birds were imported in quantity from Spain and shot down still blind and dazed by the sudden glare on release from their wooden hutches. Some managed to escape. Others, hit but not killed, would fly inland. Crippled and horribly injured yet still trusting in mankind, they hopped around the café tables in search of crumbs. The pastime was particularly favoured by English visitors – the Duke of Hamilton was one of the original members of the pigeon committee – and, thanks to the example of these sanguinary milords, the *tir aux pigeons* was soon a stylish meeting-place.

The reputation of Monte Carlo was sent spinning aloft by a visit of the Prince of Wales. Though accompanied by Princess Alexandra, he was travelling incognito as 'Captain White' – the British public still had no idea of his fondness for gambling. His visit was sedulously unreported in English newspapers, but his compatriots would hardly fail to notice the assiduity of their future sovereign at the baccara table. Other distinguished visitors about this time were the Emperor Francis Joseph, King Oscar of Sweden, King Leopold of Belgium, and the Russian grand dukes Serge, Paul, Peter and Alexis. Some of the richest players came from South America. Beginning with a spectacular win, one Brazilian lost so steadily for the rest of his stay that the weekly takings of the bank topped three hundred thousand francs. Several Nice businessmen lost very heavily and, unlike the Brazilian, it nearly ruined them. Bankruptcy would have made a scandal and stirred up fresh attacks in the press; Blanc paid back all their losses on condition that they never set foot again in the casino.

1872 was a record year at Homburg too. No one would have thought that the kursaal was under sentence of death. The social life of the little spa was as brilliant as ever and only when the summer season came to an end did a change in the quality of the clientèle become noticeable. The rich aristocrats who never staked less than the maximum were succeeded by sturdy and brutal punters who became frenzied at the loss of a florin. As the year approached its end the unlucrative crowd grew larger until the management became scared by the thought of a riot. On Sunday 29 December it was decided to end play that very evening and without notice – that is two days before the decree of abolition came into force – and those who arrived on Monday morning to be in at the kill found the kursaal locked and barred and proclamations of closure pasted all over the walls. The inside resembled a bankrupt hotel. Staff went about clanking keys. Chairs were piled up on the long gaming-tables; it was as though an auction sale was about to begin.

The sale took place. The theatre, frescoed by Viotti of Milan and Conti of Munich, was still stuck with posters announcing the last appearance of Patti in *La Somnambula*. The Salle Japonaise, where Chevet of Paris used to preside over the *table d'hôte*; the gas works; the bath house and the administrative offices – all these were put up for auction and bought by the municipality within a few days. It was a bitter blow to Blanc, but one which he could easily survive. His fortune was now reckoned at sixty million francs and, besides, he still had Monte Carlo. With the closing of the German casinos it would have the monopoly of all European gambling. The Belgian casinos had already been suppressed and the only surviving competitor, Saxon-les-Bains in Switzerland, was under sentence.

7
THE
YEARS OF
PROSPERITY

The croupiers were a strange medley of men. Some were ruined gamblers who had been taken into Blanc's service; others he had trained from their youth; yet others had been recommended by influential patrons. Their numbers and their skill were augmented now by a body of tried veterans from Homburg.

Each roulette table was supervised by a *chef de partie*, enthroned in a high chair and assisted by a *sous-chef*. The middle of the table was reserved for four croupiers, two at each side, who took turns which lasted about a quarter of an hour each in spinning the wheel; and at either end of the table an apprentice dealt with the stakes. Each trente-et-quarante table was staffed by a similar team. These were better paid than their roulette colleagues: their task was a more exacting one and called for lightning mental calculation as opposed to mere manual dexterity. Each *chef de partie* at trente-et-quarante was paid a monthly salary of seven hundred francs, whereas his opposite number at roulette got five hundred; the *tailleur* who dealt the cards at the former game earned from four hundred to six hundred francs a month, and the pay of the croupiers who spun the roulette wheel varied from two hundred and fifty francs to four hundred. They were thus sufficiently well paid not to be tempted by fraudulent practice or bribery but, to make doubly sure, they were under strict orders to keep their hands, when they were lying idle, resting on the table in full view of the public and the jackets of their suits were specially made without pockets as an additional precaution. Hanky-panky was virtually impossible.

But, however needed – and they often were – similar measures could not be brought to bear on the gamblers themselves. By this time, in addition to real money, two-franc counters were also in use. Made of copper and the same diameter as forty-sou pieces, but slightly thinner, they were stamped on one side with the words *Cercle de Monaco*, on the other with their value. Blanc had originally put 200,000 of these in circulation. But early in 1873 he found the number had inexplicably risen to 300,000, the increase being due to counterfeits which were traced to a gang in La Turbie. So the counters were done away with, the minimum stake was raised to five francs and a new system of entrance cards was introduced, each card bearing the holder's name. Blanc hoped to discourage the poorer gamblers and keep crooks out. He could afford to be difficult about his clientèle and he was more concerned with a high standard than with numbers.

The bank's reserves were more than two million francs, so that big individual wins were no longer a serious threat. On hearing of the impending arrival of such a famous gambler as 'The Maltese', who always sat down to play with a million francs in ready cash, Blanc merely took the precaution of sending to Paris for additional funds. What worried him more, though they could not all be attributed to the casino, was the growing number of suicides along the coast. In October a Pole named Felix Koniescko shot himself on the premises after losing his last penny. Fortunately he did not kill himself – in fact he had clearly had no intention of doing so, having merely given himself a flesh wound in the thigh – but he achieved his purpose, which was to attract the attention and the sympathy of the management. He was taken to the Hôtel de Paris; the best doctors looked after him at the casino's expense; and when he had recovered he was given his fare home.

The *viatique* – viaticum, or journey money – was an innovation which Blanc had introduced at Homburg. It was granted to any patron who could prove that he was genuinely stranded as a result of his losses. Monte Carlo had a better reputation in this respect than Saxon-les-Bains, where the business was conducted in 'niggardly and Helvetic style': ruined gamblers were left to fend for themselves. Sometimes, when a *décavé* did not return home even after being given the means, Blanc would pension him off for life on condition that he never attempted to re-enter the gaming rooms. These payments averaged fifteen hundred francs a day, but they were good publicity for the casino and, together with sub-scriptions to local charities and subsidies to the Nice carnival and the race-course, they were only a minute fraction of the company's expenses. These were now three million francs a year, but since the yearly takings had increased to eight million there was still a healthy margin.

The prosperity of Monte Carlo was in sharp contrast with the plight of France. The new republic was still heavily burdened with war taxes; there was not even enough cash to finish the Opera House started during the latter days of the Empire. On 24 March 1874, a law authorized the Ministry of Public Works to borrow from commercial companies or private individuals. Seizing this chance of winning further favour with the French government, Blanc immediately came forward with 4,900,000 francs – the entire sum needed. Not only did he receive six per cent interest on the loan, he had also earned the thanks of President MacMahon and persuaded him to increase the number of trains between Paris and Monaco. The flow of visitors and the profits rose accordingly.

Besides the four big Monte Carlo hotels, the principality con-tained two hundred smaller inns and furnished homes for letting. The value of the Condamine – six hundred thousand francs in 1860 – was now more than eight million, and building lots were as dear as locations in Baiae during the reign of the Caesars. Land near the casino gardens was not to be had for less than 150 francs a square metre. There were so many English, both residents and visitors, that the bishop of Gibraltar, whose diocese included the South of France, applied to Prince Charles for permission to build an English church. On the advice of the Pope the application was turned down, and the refusal led to a campaign against the casino which lasted several years. The bishop's first move was a pastoral

letter which the clergy of the English churches on the Riviera were
to read to their congregations during Lent:

> Gambling has already driven many respectable families from
> Nice and its neighbourhood. Unless public authority interposes
> to arrest this growing evil, the bright, picturesque and genial
> shores of the Mediterranean will be condemned as unfit places of
> sojourn for English families. It is probable that few, if any,
> habitual gamblers attend worship in our English churches, and
> it is not so much the gamblers themselves whom I have in my
> thoughts as those members of your congregations who, without
> supposing that they are doing any wrong, visit Monte Carlo
> either to hear the music, or to admire the scenery, or to gratify
> their curiosity of seeing whatever is to be seen, or to accompany
> friends who are bent on having a day's amusement. Ask those
> persons to consider the mischief which, unconsciously, they are
> doing. Remind them that if such an establishment existed in
> England they would never dream of being seen near the place.
> Tell them that it is by the spoils taken from the casual visitors,
> even more than by those taken from habitual players, that the
> establishment is supported. Even though they may not be
> enticed by gambling, they are sharing an amusement supplied by
> money lost at the gaming tables; they are giving the place the
> countenance and support of their presence; they are making it
> respectable, adding to its attractions, hiding its true colours, and
> so decoying others to their ruin.

No doubt the bishop was sincere in his opposition to gambling,
but if his opinion of Monte Carlo had always been as bad as his
pastoral letter suggested, his parishioners must have been surprised that he ever thought of building a church there. He over-
stated his case by alleging that the patrons of the casino were so
hardened that no one paid any attention when a gambler blew his
brains out in front of them 'only the other day': presumably an
allusion to Koniescko's farcical gesture three years before. But the
story was taken up by the British press:

> What of the suicides at Monaco and its neighbourhood – deaths
> registered oftentimes as 'accidents' but which could be more

truly described as 'Murdered by Monte Carlo'? There is no lack of *chroniques scandaleuses* on the subject, and yet the world seldom hears of the 'fatal accidents' that occur within a dozen miles of the little principality. The *Journal Officiel de Monaco* suppresses them as far as it can, and, where a suicide does come to light, it has been occasioned by 'family affairs'. The Government and Secretary of State, the police and officials, are instructed to conceal any little untoward event of this kind – of course they do, for Monte Carlo supports Monaco, and so Monaco whitewashes Monte Carlo, and the local press of Nice, Cannes, etc. are in the pay of the establishment – they never tell of the death's-head fruits of the gaming house. But in 1873 at least eight suicides were caused by gambling, and last year four suicides in one week can be proved. There is a Tarpeian rock at Monaco, which has obtained the sobriquet of *'le bastion des décavés'*, so frequent have been the suicides therefrom . . .

The evidence was not as sound as its authors affected to believe. In 1873 more than 186,000 people visited Monte Carlo, so even if the figure of eight suicides that year is correct, the suicide rate for the principality was only just over 0.004 per cent: less than half that of Great Britain today. By basing their objection on this mathematico-religious argument, the bishop and his fellow-critics of the casino were therefore no more convincing than if they had voiced their condemnation of roulette on the grounds that the numbers of the wheel add up to 666, the number of the Beast in the Book of Revelations. At any rate, in spite of the episcopal injunction, the British came to Monte Carlo in droves, and some of them, far from being ruined and reduced to suicide, derived a handsome profit from their visit. Of these the most successful was a North Country engineer by the name of Joseph Jaggers.

Unlike the big gamblers who preferred to stake on even chances at trente-et-quarante on account of the slightly more favourable odds, Jaggers concentrated exclusively on roulette and backed nothing but certain carefully chosen numbers at one specific table. He started with a very small sum, yet at the end of his first day he had won three hundred and fifty thousand francs. During the next three the sum grew to one and a half million. The achievement naturally attracted Blanc's attention, and Jaggers was kept under discreet but constant surveillance. It was the inspectors' task to study the method used by any big winner in case of trickery or from dread of an infallible system: a bogey which had always haunted casino proprietors. But Jaggers's method did not fit in with any of the known systems, all which nearly were based on even chances. He only backed numbers which he seemed to choose at random, and with inexplicable success.

But his luck was due to no system and still less to chance. Jaggers's experience of manufacturing spindles for use in the Lancashire cotton mills had taught him that no machine was technically perfect: faults, however slight, were bound to occur, even in so precise an instrument as a roulette wheel; and these faults, in their turn, were bound to cause certain numbers to appear more frequently than the rest. He had evolved the theory at home and decided to test it at Monte Carlo. Before embarking on play he engaged half a dozen clerks for a week with instructions to record every single number which came up at each of the six tables during that time. The eventual figures bore out his theory by showing that at one particular table certain numbers came up with unusual frequency. He had then sat down at that table and backed them.

In due course it dawned on the casino directors that Jaggers's success must be due to some defect in the wheel of the table at which he habitually played. They exchanged it overnight for one from another table and next morning Jaggers started laying stakes in his usual manner and lost over half his winnings before realizing that he had been outwitted. It was only a momentary setback. For a man with his technical knowledge and trained eye it was easy to spot the defective wheel – through a tiny scratch, perhaps, or some other blemish invisible to others – and no sooner had he tracked it down to the table where it had been moved than he resumed his run of success and won nearly two million francs in the course of the next few days. Once again the directors took action. Within forty-eight hours a completely new set of roulette wheels was installed, with separate component parts which were interchanged every night, so that each day's play started with what was virtually a newly constructed wheel at every table, and even Jaggers had to acknowledge defeat. Realizing he had been thwarted, for good this time, he had the sense to stop playing and leave with his winnings intact.

This was the biggest single coup so far recorded, and from then on Blanc made sure that the wheels, besides being changed every day, were also checked with a spirit-level to make certain that they were absolutely flush with the table and perfectly horizontal; as a further precaution, the croupiers were told to spin the ball in the opposite direction to the wheel and at a speed which made it go seven or even nine times round before it landed in one of the thirty-seven compartments. Since this measure made it physically impossible to spin the ball in such a way as to land it in a pre-determined compartment, there was no scope for a dishonest croupier at roulette. But although a crooked dealer at trente-et-quarante could still manipulate the cards, it was many years before anyone on the Monte Carlo staff was bribed into cheating.

Blanc had always looked older than his age; by now he had grown almost senile in appearance. The inherent perplexities of his business had strained his nerves and aggravated the chronic asthma from which he suffered, and he was increasingly aware of unfriendly criticism. His crusty manner, rumour said, was a mask under which he attempted to hide the cynical scorn he felt, especially for his staff and for the army of secret agents who allegedly would not stop at murder at his behest. He knew – who better? – how grossly exaggerated these rumours were, but they gnawed at his conscience and bred feelings of guilt. In April 1876 he fell seriously ill with bronchitis and ceased to take an active part in the running of the casino; it was entrusted to his faithful lieutenants, Wagatha and Stemmler. His professional success no longer gave him any pleasure, but later that year he had the joy of seeing Louise, his elder daughter, married to Prince Constantine Radziwill.

He had not consented to the marriage at once. Though flattered that a prince should have asked for his daughter's hand, he feared the young man might be an ordinary fortune-hunter. He engaged a confidential agent in Paris to inquire into his financial situation and way of life, and the report, beginning with his living quarters, was not reassuring: 'The family occupies the first storey. On the ground floor there is a grocer on one side and a clothier on the other. A show-case fastened to the doorpost displays an array of false teeth and the door leads through to a squalid courtyard.' It ended with a questionnaire which Blanc had asked the agent to fill in: '1. Fortune: non-existent. 2. Morality: good, excellent. 3. Character: good, excellent. 4. Family: good. 5. Politics: ——. 6. Physique: unhealthy, lungs rather weak. 7. Intelligence: ——. 8. Disposition: good, especially towards his younger brother who gambles'.

Hardly the picture of a perfect son-in-law, but charm outweighed the shortcomings and Blanc gave his consent. During the winter season, the whole of fashionable Paris was to be seen at Monte Carlo, but on the day of the wedding all Monte Carlo was in Paris and 'among those present at the magnificent and impressive ceremony were many who had involuntarily contributed to the bride's fortune, especially among the Russian families related to the Radziwills, such as the Trubetzkoys, Wittgensteins and Branickis.'

On his return, Blanc was once more beset by harassment and anxiety. Although he had subscribed five thousand francs towards the Nice carnival which he had helped to make famous, the municipal authorities showed their gratitude by constructing some grotesque effigies of him and his associates which they threatened, unless he made a further substantial contribution, to parade through the streets during the festivities. He was also concerned about the international situation. Hostilities between Russia and Turkey would seriously jeopardize the fortunes of the casino. In spite of all this, the profits in 1876 were almost five million francs. But by this time he was in no state to appreciate them. His health, going steadily downhill, drove him back to his favourite wateringplace at Loèche-les-Bains, and here, on 27 July 1877 at the age of seventy-one, he died.

The enormous sum he left – about eighty-eight million francs – provided fresh ammunition for the critics of Monte Carlo and revived hatred and envy among his personal foes, so that even after his death scurrilous stories and spiteful epigrams abounded. Most of them were in far worse taste than harmless plays on his name – '*Essayez rouge, essayez noir. C'est toujours Blanc qui gagne,*' etc. (This was the sort of remark which, in his younger days, he might have made himself, and indeed, it has been attributed to him.) His will was characteristically clear and concise. The bulk of his estate went to his wife and most of the rest was divided equally between his two daughters and his son Edmond, each of whom received 4,200 shares in the business: they were worth nearly five thousand francs each. The remainder went to two illegitimate sons, called Charles and Camille; they received 900 and 100 shares apiece. His confidential secretary, Antoine Bertora, got 900, and 800 went to a Monsieur Jandau. The prince of Monaco still held his original 400 shares.

Meanwhile play went on as usual, and during the week after Blanc's death the casino lost 640,000 francs. Many critics of gambling and many in the superstitious world of the gamblers affected to regard this as an omen. But the profits soon rose again to their normal figure and the casino, though temporarily overcast by mourning, regained its usual buoyancy. A few months later the future looked rosier than ever, for at the end of the year the only other surviving casino in Europe, Saxon-les-Bains, was closed for good and Monte Carlo's monopoly was complete.

8

THE
HOSTILE
PRESS

The mantle descended on the shoulders of Marie Blanc. As the principal shareholder in the company and widow of the founder, her position was one of command, but she preferred to stay in the wings and direct things from off stage. Antoine Bertora, who had been made a papal count, assumed nominal control, with Henri Wagatha as his lieutenant.

During the early months of 1878 the Russo-Turkish war had a damaging effect: the fighting kept the grand dukes and their reckless fellow-countrymen away from Monte Carlo. But the end of hostilities led to a fresh upsurge and the year beat all previous records – gross profits of over ten million francs against an expenditure of nearly six. As a direct result, a theatre began to go up. Until then the casino had possessed only a small and low-ceilinged concert room, in which it was impossible to cram its growing audiences. Blanc had seen the need for a larger and more splendid building, and he had already commissioned Charles Garnier for the work. Being the architect of the Paris Opera House which might never have been completed but for Blanc's generous loan, Garnier was under a heavy obligation. On the death of his benefactor he had submitted his plans to Madame Blanc and they had been accepted. In April 1878 the foundations were laid.

The work went on night and day all through the summer. In the warm weather, open-air concerts entertained the visitors and cheered up the workmen as well; the flare of the masons' torches backed the illuminations on the makeshift stage and the sounds of engine and hammer counterpointed the notes of the orchestra. A bold outline was taking shape under the cloak of the scaffolding, and when it was stripped away two tall towers were revealed, each surmounted by a cupola and a lantern. These striking features, which resembled campanili or minarets, seemed rather purposeless and incongruous at first glance, but they were visible from far out at sea and they soon came to be as closely identified with Monte Carlo as Big Ben with London or Notre Dame with Paris.

Though the general design was Garnier's, he summoned a swarm of collaborators and assistants and gave them free rein with the detail. He even took it into his head to set artists to work at skills other than their own. Sarah Bernhardt, for instance, was invited to contribute an allegorical statue called 'Song', and its fellow, 'Dance', was entrusted to Gustave Doré; both were set up in niches overlooking the terrace. Hastily executed to be ready for the opening, they were moulded in clay, cast in plaster and then given a protective coat of paint which the sun soon cracked and blistered, and in a short time both of them looked stricken with galloping eczema. In the auditorium, too, Garnier had allowed his artists to run riot. The vaulted roof was supported by four giant bronze and gold caryatids and the two naked young men perched on the narrow ledge immediately below them looked freshly risen from the bath. The door of the prince's box was lit by twin candelabra in the form of Nubian slaves and another two caryatids in Florentine bronze flanked the entrance from the atrium into the theatre. Madame Blanc was afraid that the profusion of gilded ornamentation – the friezes, the garlands, the panoplies and the frescoes – would only serve to remind customers of all the money they had lost.

For everyone except Prince Charles, who by this time was almost totally blind, the gala opening on 25 January 1879 was in every way a dazzling event. Sarah Bernhardt recited an appropriate metrical paean and Garnier was decorated with the Cross of the Order of Saint Charles. At first the theatre was thought to be too large for the casino, but it turned out such a success that soon the casino was too small for the theatre and additions and alterations were put in train. The Salle Mauresque became the atrium and next year Garnier extended the capacities of the main gaming room by adding a new and spacious chamber.

The gardens were redesigned. Homburg had taught Blanc the value of somewhere pleasant to sit or stroll within safe range of the casino's lure. When Monte Carlo was still in its infancy, he had imported rare trees and plants from many countries. Now fully grown, their richness and variety gave rise to ecstatic outbursts, especially among visitors from the North:

> The deciduous trees of Europe intertwine with their bark-shedding Australian congenors; the palm trees of Asia and Africa nod their feathered heads to their kindred from over the Atlantic; the Norfolk Island araucaria stands stem to stem with the Washingtonea gigantea of the Yosemite Valley, and here and there, quite out of line and spared by the dragooning of horti-culture, thrives a gnarled olive or venerable carob-tree, or some other survivor of the ancient denizens of the soil.

Hot-houses had been built and a variety of flowerbeds laid out. But the beds had fallen into neglect. Rare plants and precious ferns had withered and died: they used to be watered, it emerged, from the washing-up sinks of the Hôtel de Paris. All this was changed and later visitors, among them Osbert Sitwell – then a schoolboy on holiday – marvelled at:

> the elaborate gardens and *tapis-vert*, in which every blade of grass ranked as elsewhere would a flower, and had to be watered separately, whereas each flower was common as a blade of grass, albeit carefully brushed every morning and sheltered every night. Even the leaves of the palm-trees appeared to be clipped like poodles, and numbered, the flower-beds to be creations as artificial as the large hats of the women seated by them, listening to the music of *Sole Mio* being played by a band in a café nearby.

The casino still had its enemies, and their attacks were beginning to take a more violent form. On 24 April 1880, at ten o'clock at night, a bomb exploded under the clock in the main gaming room. Several players were wounded by flying glass and panic broke out.

There was a rush for the doors, which became jammed with a seething and struggling mass. Others jumped out of the windows in terror and fell in the roadway helter-skelter. Keeping their heads, the croupiers remained on guard at the tables in case of an attempted robbery. If this was the motive behind the outrage, it was successfully foiled by the resolute casino staff and also, perhaps, for another reason. When the gas lights had gone out, there was still a faint gleam from the oil lamps which were lit every evening in the event of just such an emergency (they are set up there still in case of an electricity failure) and they threw enough light to unnerve the criminals who must have been counting on darkness. Investigations indicated that the bomb had been concealed under a hat left on a mantelpiece. The owner of the hat was never discovered and the incident was soon forgotten; but after that, no one was allowed to take a hat, a coat or a parcel into the gaming rooms, and the precaution holds good today.

Later in the same year, Madame Blanc married off her second daughter, another Marie, to Prince Roland Bonaparte. He was a nephew of the Charles Lucien who had once nearly broken the bank at Homburg and this time there had been no need to inquire into the suitor's prospects: everybody knew that the young man had nothing but his name. His father had served as a mercenary in Colombia and Egypt and Italy before he finally married the daughter of a plumber; but Madame Blanc, herself the daughter of a cobbler and, for all her German parentage, an ardent Francophil, had no objection to a union which linked her to the French imperial family. But she was not to enjoy this enviable relationship for long. She died without warning, and at the comparatively early age of forty-seven, on 25 July 1881, while she was staying at her country house in Haute Savoie.

The enormous sums involved in the sale of her jewellery at the Hôtel Drouot later that year – one pearl necklace alone fetched 360,000 francs – unleashed a further series of attacks against the casino. Another bomb exploded, this time just outside the gaming rooms; it caused even less damage than the first and it was forgotten even more quickly. The press campaign was more serious. It was launched by the newly formed International Committee for the Suppression of the Gaming Tables of Monte Carlo. Pamphlets and books against gambling began to appear not only in London and on the Riviera but all over Europe, and an alarmist headline in a local newspaper – *Vendez, vendez, actionnaires, le krach s'approche* (Sell, sell, shareholders, the crash is coming) – caused a heavy fall in the company's shares.

At the time of Madame Blanc's death the casino's capital amounted to fifteen million francs. In the following year the company was reconstituted. The capital was raised to thirty million divided into sixty thousand shares of five hundred francs each, of which the Blanc family held fifty-two thousand. At the same time François' eldest son Camille was appointed chief director.

The hostile press campaign continued and even *The Times* abandoned its usual reserve by printing the following report from Paris:

> Now that the evils of Bourse gambling are being so strikingly exemplified, the movement against that nursery of gambling, Monte Carlo, is more than ever opportune. A petition has just been presented to the French Senate from inhabitants of the coast and foreign residents or visitors, urging the Parliament and Government to put a stop to the scandal and dangers of the Monaco gaming tables. The petitioners dwell on the demoralizing influence of this place of corruption on the neighbouring town [Nice] and on visitors to the Riviera, on the throng of bad characters attracted by the gaming tables, and on the rights and obligations of France, a mere threat from whom would bring the Prince of Monaco to reason . . .

This was followed five weeks later by a second message:

> The movement against the Monaco gaming tables is evidently gaining ground in France. The Committee on Petitions will shortly report on it to the Senate and a discussion will doubtless be devoted to it . . .

It never took place. Parliamentary debate on gambling was shelved and a leader in *The Times* reported that only diplomatic

LEFT Villa Bellevue, the modest premises of Monaco's first casino, 1856.
BELOW Croupiers scanning the Nice road for prospective clients, 1860.

François Blanc, who founded the
present casino in 1863.

Prince Charles of Monaco
(1818–1889), after whom Monte
Carlo was named.

The Monte Carlo casino in the 1870s before the opera house was built.

The casino in the mid-1880s showing Garnier's twin towers.

THIS PAGE AND ABOVE RIGHT Sem's caricatures of the Monte Carlo
gaming set.

BELOW Interior of the casino at the turn of the century.

The Spélugues promontory in 1863.

The same view, showing present-day Monte Carlo.

LEFT Prince Albert of Monaco
(1848–1922).
ABOVE Princess Alice, Prince Albert's
American wife.
BELOW Camille Blanc, François Blanc's
illegitimate son, who ran the casino
from 1881 to 1923.
BELOW LEFT Mata Hari, whose career as
a spy was confirmed at Monte Carlo.

Sir Basil Zaharoff in the twenties.

BELOW Aristotle Onassis, who gave Monte Carlo a new lease of life in 1954.
LEFT Prince Rainier and Princess Grace, the ruling sovereigns.

action was to be taken although, the article continued, somewhat inconsistently:

> But, for all that, it is plain that the casino is seriously threatened . . . A score of tables are in constant use from morning till midnight, and hundreds of deluded persons from all parts of Europe are occupied continually in the fascinating but hopeless struggle against the inevitable law by which the Bank must win . . . It is natural that a good deal of indignation should have been excited by this spectacle of a practice forbidden by the laws of every state in Europe brazening it out at Monte Carlo . . . Every year the crowds of English and French visitors are increasing; and it is not mainly for the gambling that they go.

Among them was Queen Victoria, who was staying at Menton that winter. She drove over to Monaco, walked up to the Rock and enjoyed the view. She pointedly failed to call on the prince and expressed her views on gambling by returning a bouquet of flowers which the casino directors had sent in the hope of luring her for a few minutes to Monte Carlo.

The bishop of Gibraltar reopened hostilities with another letter. This time the physical climate of Monte Carlo came under fire alongside the moral:

> A few English families on the recommendation of their medical advisers, as I am informed, have lately taken villas or apartments at Monte Carlo. Such recommendation, I am sure, must have been given in ignorance. No physician, who cares for the moral welfare of his patients, would send them to Monte Carlo if he knew the real character of the place . . . I know that I am not exaggerating when I say that at Monte Carlo is to be found the very scum of all Europe. None can live there without jostling daily against the reckless, the unprincipled, the abandoned of both sexes. No lad, no modest woman should venture within the precincts of the establishment. Some people are now building an English church as a commercial speculation at Monaco and have asked me to give the enterprise my sanction. Clergymen also from time to time have expressed a wish to conduct services

there, and have applied to me for a licence. But as I have no desire to attract members of my Church and country to this scene of temptation and iniquity, and have always maintained that persons of right principle not only should avoid the place as a residence, but should never be drawn by their curiosity even to pay it a visit, I have declined such requests.* The only ground on which a physician could justify himself in recommending families to reside there, is the supposed excellence of its climate. But, as a matter of fact, Monte Carlo enjoys no exceptional advantages of climate which are not enjoyed by other health resorts along the Riviera ... Physicians at home ought to be made aware that there are no level walks at Monte Carlo suitable for invalids. The old picturesque town of Monaco itself is situated on a promontory much exposed to the wind, and is, therefore, very unfit for persons suffering from weakness of the chest ...

These views were echoed by a Dr Drysdale, who voiced his opinion in the *Pall Mall Gazette*:

I am glad to see that there is at length some prospect of the gambling tables at Monte Carlo being closed. I am a medical man practising at Mentone, which is in perilous proximity (only a quarter of an hour by rail), and I have several times had the mortification of seeing patients sink into their graves who would have recovered – had they not been enticed into that most pernicious of all forms of excitement, gambling. I know of no more painful sight than that of a consumptive with his temples throbbing, his eyes eagerly glittering, and a burning spot on each cheek, stretching out a trembling hand to place his stake ...

The prince was tarred with the same brush as the directors of the casino, and *The Times* again called for direct action against him:

Monaco is in reality neither an independent state nor a principality. It is simply an estate, and its ruler is a French nobleman who greatly abuses privileges founded upon the curious history of his patch of soil. If he chose to shelter pirates in his little harbour instead of croupiers on the rocky slopes to the eastward,

* The church was duly built none the less.

no one would think of setting up his nominal independence as a reason for respecting his domestic situation . . .

But this argument had no effect on him, nor did it alarm Camille Blanc and his associates unduly. As a precaution, they set a rumour afloat that if the casino came to be closed, the prince might cede his territory to Germany or to the United States, and the mere threat of foreign troops stationed on the Rock or foreign vessels anchored in the harbour was enough to dissuade the French government from action.

Only one small voice was raised against all these virulent attacks. Amid the croaking unanimity of his fellow-peers and the compatriot signatories of the anti-gambling petition, Lord Ashburton sounded a high and heartening note. He pointed out with great common sense and some prolixity that neither France, with night and day gambling in her countless private clubs, nor Italy with her state lottery, could decently strike a pious attitude towards Monte Carlo. He concluded:

I regret very much that the immense influence of *The Times* should be employed to support the agitation fostered in England by amiable enthusiasts who divide their energies between promoting the interests of animals and restricting the enjoyments of their fellow-creatures . . . [an agitation] only kept up on the Continent by the rapacious proprietors of hotels, lodging houses and gambling clubs on the Riviera, who are furious against Monaco because reasonable persons prefer risking their money there at fair play to being fleeced out of it for the benefit, direct or indirect, of simple speculators . . .

Toleration prevailed and the campaign, especially when it was seen that envy had prompted it far more than morals, petered out. But only two years later the casino was faced with the threat of extinction from a different source. On 23 February 1887 – it happened to be Ash Wednesday – at thirty-seven minutes past five in the morning, an initial tremor heralded the earthquake which shook the whole of the Riviera. It was not violent enough to cause wholesale destruction – some houses collapsed in Nice and the gendarmerie barracks in Menton were reduced to rubble – but three hundred people in San Remo were killed while in church. They were the only dead.

In Monte Carlo the square outside the casino was thronged with masked revellers on their way home from the great Shrove Tuesday ball. The earth shook, several buildings came crashing to the ground and panic seized the crowd. The superstitious, seeing an act of God, fell on their knees and prayed for deliverance: divine judgement seemed to be upon them. Others gazed at the casino in awe; they were waiting to see it destroyed in retribution; almost hoping, perhaps . . . But, to the dismay of moralists and the anti-gambling committees, the shameless building was spared while several churches were badly damaged. The irony was noted in *The Times*:

> We can imagine the sensation that would have been caused throughout the world had the casino fallen a victim to the shock. What so appropriate as that on the first morning of Lent that home of wickedness should have been suddenly destroyed by the forces of outraged nature – should have shared the fate of Dathan and Abiram, and 'gone down quick into the pit'! Piety would have regarded the ruin as a judgement on a place that had so long tempted providence; and scepticism would have remarked that it was a singular coincidence. Fortunately, or unfortunately, the casino still stands, and the course of the roulette ball is unaltered by seismic disturbances. Yet, like the rest of the neighbourhood, Monte Carlo will be sure to suffer severely from the earthquake; for if ordinary holiday-makers are already hurrying out of Nice, superstitious and conscience-stricken amateur gamblers will be certain to rush away from Monte Carlo . . .

The prophesy was only partly fulfilled. An exodus did take place; frenzied and terrified people fought savagely for places in the train; and the shares of the company momentarily fell. But, by the time the new season began, the earthquake had been forgotten or turned into a joke and the faithful had all drifted back. One of them, the wife of a French baron who was a governor of the Bank of France, had been heard to proclaim that if she were spared by the earthquake she would devote the rest of her days to religious works, give all her winnings to charity and never set foot in Monte Carlo again. When asked if she had paid for the building of a church as she had promised, she shrugged and said that the earthquake had only been a small one . . . 'I thought half a dozen candles to the Virgin would do.'

Her fellow-guests at the Hôtel de Paris that winter were the emperor and empress of Austria and the dowager empress of Russia, the queen of Portugal, the king of Sweden, the king of Belgium and the king of Serbia. Profits rose to nearly twenty million francs and 1888 was another boom year. But on 10 September 1889, Prince Charles died and his death gave rise to anxious speculations on the attitude of his successor towards the casino. Prince Albert was a rich man: apart from the fortune he now inherited from his father there was the handsome dowry of his marriage in 1869 to Lady Mary-Victoria Douglas Hamilton, which he had retained when he divorced her five years later. Besides, a month after his father's death, he married another rich woman. The American widow of the Duc de Richelieu, *née* Alice Heine, was a great-niece of the famous poet and a direct descendant of a line of international bankers who had rivalled the Rothschilds for three generations. He was of a scientific turn; gambling bored him; and as he could afford to dispense with the one and a quarter million francs a year which had been the share of his predecessor, the casino directors feared he might cancel their concession and put them out of business.

Such at least was the pious hope of the bishop of Gibraltar. There was yet another pastoral letter comminating the place: 'The running sore which is never healed, the mephitic exhalation perpetually poisoning the atmosphere of the Riviera . . .' But the contract drawn up by Prince Charles and François Blanc was valid until 1913, and Prince Albert had no power to annul it. The casino was safe for another quarter of a century and the prince continued to accept his yearly tribute.

The enemies, having failed through government action, changed their tune and so did the hostile press. Three years previously the *Times* correspondent had been primly deploring the ostentation of the place – 'Palatial is a poor word to describe its general appearance, for no palace in the world is so wasteful, so unreflectingly sumptuous.' The same correspondent now criticized the niggardly policy of the shareholders:

> During the past few years an entire change has come over the style of conducting the casino. The society has developed a businesslike policy of the most careful and economizing character. The bountiful spirit of *largesse* which prompted all the actions of Monsier Blanc in his Homburg and early Monte Carlo administrations has been completely stifled, and in its place we find an amount of parsimoniousness worthy of the most hard-pressed dealer in second-hand wares. The older rooms are shabby, badly ventilated and uncomfortable ...

He omitted to say that only a year earlier the vestibule had been enlarged and a new gaming room completed, and that two further rooms were under construction. He then complained that the social tone – 'if such a term may be used' – was fast declining and that the players, though more numerous, were unfortunately of a lower class. He spoke of rascally fellows and horrible old harpies who lived by snatching other people's money at the tables, and he went on:

> Another change of front is that displayed towards the subservient subventioned press. For many years the administration spent large sums, varying from £10,000 to £15,000 per annum, in the purchase of silence from newspapers of this district and the payment of certain journalists for their policy of masterly inactivity regarding the doings of the casino people. Something like a hundred newspapers are in the pay of the bank, receiving *douceurs* of from £50 to £500 per annum. Last year many were placed on the retired list at half-pay, and the present management has shown defiance to all criticism by deciding to postpone indefinitely all new applications for assistance in the journalistic line ... The dodge for obtaining money from the bank by the repeated publication of fictitious suicides and other exaggerated items is practically played out; the management know that, and

they intend to face the fusillade of all fresh attacks upon the casino coffers.

While cataloguing Camille Blanc's parsimoniousness, the *Times* correspondent failed to mention his generous continuance of the viaticum which his father had instituted. He ended with the reflection that heavy gambling – 'plunging' – was a thing of the past: maximum stakes were seldom seen and the scenes of wild excitement had become few and far between.

Other reports in the British press suggested that Monte Carlo was on the wane, the future of the casino uncertain, the gambling concession unlikely to be renewed, the independence of Monaco yet to be acknowledged by the French. All this, based more on wishful thoughts than on reason, was designed to spread alarm among the shareholders. The casino administration prudently established a reserve fund for the next twenty-three years. A million francs were to be paid in yearly. If their contract were annulled at the end of that time, they would be able to liquidate their business and reimburse the shareholders with a profit.

The fear of French intervention, already remote, disappeared for ever in 1891, when the question of gambling was raised for the last time in the French Chamber. It was settled with the words: 'The Principality of Monaco is absolutely independent and its independence is recognized.'

9

A NEW
LEASE
OF LIFE

With the independence of the principality confirmed, and the concession guaranteed, a fresh spirit affected Monte Carlo. The gaming rooms were still thronged with people playing for low stakes, the 'rascally fellows and old harpies' of yesteryear had not died out, but judging by stories of the amazing wins that were bandied about all through the season, swarms of big gamblers were back as well. Many of these tales were mere fancy; others, almost certainly, were launched by the casino itself. The *Times* correspondent had to eat his words. 'Plungers', he wrote, 'are breaking the tables every day.'*

On one occasion, at a trente-et-quarante table, an Englishman staked the maximum and won fourteen times running and cleared up nearly a quarter of a million francs. At the same table, two weeks later, three Italian noblemen placed maximum stakes on red for six hours on end and were rewarded with a run of seven successful coups. Other gamblers at once began to copy the method and by the end of the day the casino had lost more than three quarters of a million. At roulette, meanwhile, a far more speculative and risky game than trente-et-quarante, an English earl

---

* In other words, they were winning so much that the reserves of gold coins which were kept at each table ran out and had to be replenished. In the interval, the table was shrouded in black crêpe – a publicity stunt which François Blanc had devised at Homburg. No losing table is 'put in mourning' nowadays: the store of counters and plaques which have taken the place of gold coins is renewed at the first sign of depletion.

won half a million francs in the space of three days. Such a feat was so rare that for a time no one could speak of anything else. Out of discretion the names of these large-scale winners were seldom revealed; also, when the facts and figures could not be fully authenticated, anonymity was best. The most famous of all vanished into the golden and nameless apotheosis of The Man Who Broke the Bank at Monte Carlo...

This deed, of course, was never done. To break the bank would have meant emptying the reserves of all the gaming tables at once; an impossible feat for any single player or even for a large syndicate with unlimited means. But to break one table once in a lifetime was memorable enough; several times in one day was more remarkable still. To do so several days running was a never-to-be-forgotten event. It is linked forever with the name of Charles Deville Wells.

He arrived in Monte Carlo bringing with him a hundred thousand francs. His looks were commonplace – he was middle-aged and of medium height, with a short black beard and a bald head – and when he entered the casino on 19 July 1891 he excited no attention until he sat down at one of the roulette tables and started to play. He conducted himself with the recklessness of a mad millionaire bent on getting rid of everything he possessed. When he rose from the table eleven hours later he was the richer by more than a quarter of a million francs. He repeated this feat on the following day, still at roulette. On the third day, after a short adverse run during which he lost fifty thousand francs, he switched to trente-et-quarante and staked in maximums until he had got back his losses. Then, reverting to roulette, he proceeded to break the table a dozen times in the course of the afternoon.

By now nobody had eyes for anything else; he was not only an intrepid gambler but also a *beau joueur* – someone who played to the gallery, that is. After his first spectacular win the casino inspectors had, as usual, kept a close watch. The management were deeply perturbed: perhaps they had another Jaggers on their hands? Wells frequently boasted of his skill as an engineer. And though the ancient chimera of an infallible system was no longer taken seriously, it was not discarded altogether. But Wells's system – apparently the *coup des trois*, which consisted of allowing the stakes to accumulate for three successive wins and then with-drawing the lot and starting again – was well known. Countless gamblers had already been ruined by it, yet he played on, doubling up to the maximum when in luck and reducing his stakes on striking an adverse run, with conspicuous and continuous success.

His method, he explained, was based on calculations which had occurred to him while he was at work on mechanical inventions, and he claimed that it was infallible but only in his hands. 'Of course,' he added, 'anyone is free to watch me play and follow my example. But average gamblers lack the courage to risk large stakes and they haven't the stamina to play eleven hours a day.' His own gave out at the end of three, but by this time he had won more than half a million francs. He transferred it at once to his bank in London and followed it.

He was back again at the start of the winter season and again another extraordinary run of luck set in. He broke a roulette table several times in the course of his first session and on the following day, 7 November, he accomplished the prodigious feat of breaking one of the trente-et-quarante tables by half past eleven in the morning, only half an hour after the casino had opened. He lost steadily for the rest of the day, but when he finished the session he was still thirty thousand up.

Once again the inspectors kept a hawk-like watch – even, to his vexation, while he was outside the casino premises – and he was pestered by fellow-gamblers down on their luck. A lady asked him in tears for a hundred and fifty thousand francs which she asserted had been included in his winnings by mistake, and a woebegone figure demanded the return of fifty thousand francs – his daughter's *dot*, he pathetically explained – which had likewise been passed to the lucky winner by mistake. These were small worries. Wells's luck still held. During his last session at the trente-et-quarante table he staked thirty maximums running and won twenty-three. He then proceeded to break the roulette table all over again. Again his winnings were promptly dispatched to his bank. This time he further showed his good sense by buying fifty thousand francs' worth of shares in the casino. Even the *Times* correspondent – albeit with reservations – could scarce forbear to cheer.

Wells returned to Monte Carlo in January next year in a magnificent steam-yacht called the *Palais Royal*. He entertained on board with splendour – one evening he had five British peers to dinner, with their wives, and a German millionaire, three American millionaires and a distinguished French diplomat – but his luck seemed to have deserted him. After breaking the table six times shortly after his arrival, he began to lose heavily and steadily. Not for an instant, however, did he alter his standard of living. The *Palais Royal* remained in harbour for the remainder of the season, the expensive dinner parties continued, and funds arrived regularly from London to make up for his losses. His wealth appeared to be limitless. He ascribed it to lucky share transactions in the City and to the success of his many inventions.

It was not until the end of the year, when he was arrested aboard the *Palais Royal* in Havre harbour, that his actual financial condition was revealed: he was reduced to such straits that he had been trying to sell the coal in the yacht's bunkers to a local merchant. But this was not the reason for his arrest. An extradition order against him had been issued by the British government, and on 17 January 1893 he appeared at Bow Street on a charge of obtaining £28,000 by false pretences. In the police court, and during his subsequent trial at the Old Bailey, the facts leading up to his activities at Monte Carlo were gradually disclosed.

The sums he had gambled with were the haul from a series of swindles. Describing himself as an inventor and civil engineer – though his only invention was a musical skipping-rope which had not sold well – he had talked a number of gullible backers into parting with their money by promising them handsome profits once his ingenious mechanical devices had been put on the market. From one victim alone – Catherine Phillimore, sister of the judge Sir Walter Phillimore – he extracted more than £18,000. Even the yacht had been acquired by fraud. He needed it, he said, to test an apparatus for saving fuel on coal-burning ships. The funds to make up for his gambling losses were not due to his astute investments, as he had claimed. They had been sent by Miss Phillimore and his other victims in answer to his telegrams – dispatched from Menton or Nice but never from Monte Carlo – asking for more cash in order to repair the fuel-saving device which, as he explained, kept breaking down.

He got eight years and by the time he came out he had sunk into obscurity. But his feats at the gaming tables were still being celebrated in a song. Thanks to Charles Coburn, it was the rage of the London music-halls, then it blazed through the provinces and America and it isn't quite dead yet:

> As I walk along in the Bois de Boulong with an independent air,
> You can hear the girls declare, he must be a millionaire,
> Oh, and then they sigh and wish to die,
> And they turn and wink the other eye,
> It's the man who broke the bank at Monte Carlo.

It was not the end of Wells's career. In 1906, under a false name and working in partnership with an unfrocked clergyman, he was arrested for fraud and sentenced to three more years' hard labour. It transpired that he had used his Monte Carlo winnings and much of the money obtained through false pretences to buy himself a number of annuities; so, although he was adjudged bankrupt with liabilities of £35,000 while he was in prison, he was potentially quite affluent still. This astute measure had fended off destitution and provided for his old age. He was again sentenced for fraud, in Paris this time, and served five years in a French prison; and on his release the government allowed him twenty-five thousand francs a year to keep alive on in order to get as much as possible from his annuities for his creditors' benefit. He was able to end his days in comparative comfort and free from financial worries. He died in 1929 at the age of eighty-five.

The success of the song about Wells's great triumph made Monte Carlo doubly famous. Everything prospered. The receipts in 1892 were nearly twenty-five million – again a million up on the year before. In 1893 they were more than twenty-four million and the 500-franc shares of 1884 were quoted at a little over 2,500 francs. The Blanc family still held most of these, and no one holding less than two hundred took part in the shareholders' meetings. It was now decided to split up the existing sixty thousand shares into fifths and redistribute them at their original price of five hundred francs so that the capital of the company might be increased and the management, hitherto in the hands of no more than a dozen or so, extended to include many more.

Since Wells, there had been no big winners. *The Times* mentioned a young Russian who 'succeeded in taking out £4,000 on Friday, the last day of the financial year; but he went back yesterday, All Fools' Day, and lost it all.' The report continued:

The season's play has rather been characterized by the attendance at the tables of an ever-increasing multitude of small gamblers, a class which the management likes to see best, for, with their limited capital, they are unable to make any stand against a run of bad luck. They lose their money rapidly and make room for others. Another striking feature of the gambling rooms this season has been the increase in rowdyism and rascaldom. Scarcely a day passes without some quarrel over the stakes, and the casino has certainly never harboured such a gang of thieves as that which practised upon the pockets of people standing round the tables during carnival time.

The season was marked by a conspicuous decline in the number of British visitors. The Americans and Russians remained more or less static, and German excursionists were vastly on the increase. 'As a rule undesirable from the decorative point of view', they were divided up into small groups with a typical Teutonic thoroughness and each group had a leader entrusted with the communal funds who placed the stakes on behalf of the rest. These groups contributed absolutely nothing to the social level of the rooms and made the overcrowding worse.

While welcoming the multitude who provided the bulk of the casino's takings, the directors knew they risked losing the rich, fashionable and aristocratic world which had made Monte Carlo such a focus of elegance and luxury. Something had to be done to discriminate between high life and the rabble, and Camille Blanc decided to establish what he called the *cercle privé* in a small upstairs room. It was to be a select institution to which men alone were admitted. There were three tables for trente-et-quarante and one for roulette, and play started after the tables downstairs had closed and went on until very late and in much greater comfort than in the public rooms. Most of the players knew each other; the atmosphere was much more intimate and conducive to high stakes. It was rather like a club where the members were all in league against the bank. From their point of view the *cercle privé* was a boon, especially since the ratio of three trente-et-quarante tables to one of roulette was considerably in their favour. Most of them were experienced gamblers and the bank was proportionately more vulnerable: on one evening it lost more than had ever before been lost by the casino in a single day. But this in no way affected the company's overall takings; they climbed steadily all through the next five years.

Reports of the bank being 'broken' again – this time by the earl of Rosslyn – gave a fresh boost to the casino. An odd but reliable eye-witness – Sir Hiram Maxim, the inventor of the famous machine-gun – tells us what really happened:

Lord Rosslyn and Mr Sam Lewis (a well-known money-lender) approached a trente-et-quarante table and each staked a maximum of twelve thousand francs upon black; in fact I never saw Mr Lewis bet on anything except black, and always at trente-et-quarante, where the percentage against him was the lowest. Black came up and the bank paid these two gentlemen twenty-four thousand francs. Again each staked a maximum, the cards were dealt again, and another twenty-four thousand was paid out by the bank. After about seven consecutive wins, it was said that the bank had technically been broken; a bell was rung, and a factor of the bank approached with considerable ceremony; a demand was made, also with a considerable amount of ceremony, for more money; again with a considerable amount of ceremony it was delivered, and the play went on, black coming up every time. The bank was again broken; more money was sent for, more ceremony. This time there was great excitement; hundreds of people were crowding about the table, and everybody that could stake a louis staked on black, and black continued to come up for seventeen times. Then on the eighteenth coup, which was red, Lord Rosslyn and Mr Lewis each lost twelve thousand francs. This was the longest run that I ever witnessed at Monte Carlo. However, my suspicions were excited; I did not believe for a moment that the bank had actually been broken. I knew that there had been a great deal of play during the day, and that the winnings at this particular table must have been very heavy indeed. I therefore remained to see the money taken from the table, when I found it was exactly as I had expected; there was at least a peck of large bank notes. It had not been necessary for the bank to send for money at all, this had only been done for effect.

Their luck did not last. Next morning Lord Rosslyn lost consistently, both at trente-et-quarante and roulette, and by two in the afternoon he had to cash a cheque in order to continue playing. As for Sam Lewis, he confessed that he had lost 'enough money to build a casino'.

Another spectacular win was made soon afterwards by Woolf Joel, the South African millionaire, and the Australian financier Frank Gardiner. They won on red at trente-et-quarante no fewer than twelve times running, and since they too both staked the maximum each time, between them they won over a quarter of a million francs in a few minutes. They gave a celebration dinner at the Savoy in London which was known as the 'All-Red Dinner': the walls were draped from ceiling to carpet in the winning colour and even the waiters were in red. There were only red wines and the menu consisted of Prawns, Queues de Langouste en Aspic, Crème Portugaise, Saumon à la Nantua, Mousse au Jambon, Filet de Boeuf aux Tomates Farcies, Choux-Rouges Braisés, Poularde à la Cardinal, Canard Sauvage au Sang, Salade de Betterave, and Mousse aux Fraises. A few months later Joel was shot dead in his office at Johannesburg by one of his employees.

By 1898 the initiates of the *cercle privé* had increased to such an extent that the room could no longer hold them. It was transferred to the large house which had formerly belonged to Madame Blanc and reconstituted as an even more exclusive society, to be known henceforth as the International Sporting Club. Baccara was introduced as a new attraction and, to qualify, a visitor had to belong to a recognized club in his own country and produce a receipt to show that he had paid his yearly subscription. Shortly after its inauguration the Sporting Club was the scene of a comparatively rare event: a swindle involving a member of the casino staff. Four Italian gamblers bribed a *tailleur* at one of the trente-et-quarante tables to arrange a pack of cards in a certain sequence and insert it among the other packs which comprised the 'shoe'.* The *tailleur* could easily hide the doctored pack up the sleeve of his dinner-jacket before going on duty; the problem was to slip it into the 'shoe' without being spotted by the *chef de partie*, the *sous-chef* and the other croupiers at the table, not to mention prowling inspectors or a chance spectator. But a combination of audacity, dexterity, synchronization and psychological insight achieved the almost impossible feat.

At a given moment between two 'shoes', one of the Italians asked the *chef de partie* to change him a 500-franc note. As the twenty-five louis were handed to him he pretended to fumble and dropped the gold coins on the floor with a crash. Everyone looked round, including the officials of the table who instinctively helped him to gather them up. In this fraction of a second the *tailleur* inserted his 'sandwich' of cards; or rather, for lack of time, placed it on top of the other six packs. No one noticed; there was not the least suspicion that the Italian's clumsiness had been deliberate, and play was resumed. Each of the swindlers staked the maximum and won every time, until the last card of the prepared pack. Then all four of them got up and left. Their joint departure at the end of such an astonishing run of luck could hardly be a coincidence; the management's suspicions were confirmed when the 'shoe' was found to contain fifty-two extra cards. Taxed with this irregularity, the *tailleur* broke down and confessed that he had been bribed with sixty thousand francs.

Another swindle by a gang of four occurred at a chemin-de-fer table soon after, but this time with only the partial connivance of the croupier. Nothing in their appearance or bearing suggested

* For an explanation of this word, see p. 156.

they were in league. Nor, at least to begin with, was there anything to rouse suspicion in their method. They played against one another as four complete strangers might have done; each of them won or lost accordingly. At the end of four 'shoes', however, they started betting the same way and all together. Coup after coup came out in their favour, as though an extremely accurate sixth sense had enabled them to judge the odds each time the cards were dealt. The change of tactics, followed by their sudden run of luck, attracted the attention of a particularly acute and intelligent inspector. He watched them more closely, and soon it occurred to him that it might be more than a coincidence that all four of them were wearing dark glasses. There was something fishy about this, he felt, but he could not tell exactly what until he slipped on his own pair. He saw at once that the value of each relevant card was marked on the back with white specks.

The four men were obviously guilty of trickery, but their guilt had to be proved. There was no proof that they were responsible for the white specks on the cards, and no way of explaining how they had been able to mark them; and since their victims had not been the bank but their fellow-players, the finances of the casino were not affected. The management therefore decided to take no action for the time being but gave orders for the cards to be changed, and changed again at the end of every second 'shoe'. Then they examined the marked packs. They discovered that the white specks consisted of a chemical compound which made them invisible to the naked eye. Presumably the compound, hidden on the persons of the four swindlers – secreted under their fingernails, perhaps? – had enabled them to mark the cards during the run of the first four 'shoes'. It was impossible for them to repeat the trick now that the cards were changed after every second 'shoe'; it prevented them from marking enough cards for their purpose and the fact that the management had taken these precautions showed them that their scheme had been uncovered. Yet instead of heeding this warning and being content with their winnings they were foolish enough to try another swindle a few days later.

This time only one of the four was wearing dark glasses; he was not playing but standing behind the banker. The three others won heavily and the management soon understood that the man with the glasses was signalling the value of each card as it was dealt. Once again white specks were found upon the backs of the cards. Yet the crooks themselves would not have been able to mark them, for the packs were issued only when they were needed, they were carefully checked every night at the end of play and then locked up till the following day. Clearly a member of the casino staff was involved. The croupiers on duty at that table were questioned and one of them eventually admitted that he had stolen several new packs from the casino and taken them to the gang at Nice, where they had been carefully unsealed, marked with the chemical compound and sealed up again before being replaced in the safe. From here they were issued to the dishonest croupier's table, where the crooks had taken their seats.

Armed with this evidence, the directors were able to have the four men arrested and charged in the Monaco courts. It was some time before they came up for trial: the Monégasque lawyers maintained that the case should be heard in Nice, since it was there that the crime – the actual marking of the cards – had been committed. But according to the French lawyers, the marking of the cards constituted no offence; using them was the crime, and this had been committed in Monaco. This legal wrangle was somehow resolved in the end and they all received heavy sentences.

The Times, and her sister news-sheets, predicted 1913 as the year of the casino's final doom: it was the expiry date of the original concession granted to François Blanc. Prince Albert was known to disapprove of gambling and, true sportsman that he was, of pigeon-shooting still more, at least as it was practised by the crack shots at Monte Carlo. He couldn't bear them

> With their suits of elegant cut, [he wrote] thin and highly polished boots, hair dressed with sheep-like submission to the whims of fashion, fancy gloves to protect their effeminate hands from the cold, or vulgar contacts or exposure; virgin guns with neither scratch nor scar; everything about these fragile marksmen is characterless and vapid.

Apprised of the prince's scruples, Camille Blanc sought to overcome them well in advance by negotiating for an extension on terms which must have made his father groan in anguish. What he offered was no less than a bonus of ten million francs in the following year, and a further fifteen million in 1913. The casino also undertook to contribute five million francs towards the construction of the harbour, six hundred thousand a year towards the expenses of the theatre, plus whatever sums were needed for the laying of new roads and the maintenance of those already in existence. Finally, the prince's annual subsidy of one and a quarter million francs was to be raised to one and three quarter million in 1908, two million in 1918, two and a quarter million in 1928 and two and a half million in 1938. Such an offer was not to be refused. Trampling on his scruples, the prince signed a new concession which prolonged the life of the company to 1948. The future of the casino was assured for at least two generations. This strengthened the position of Camille Blanc in the company. As chief director he could leave all the administrative duties to subordinates and concentrate exclusively on finance.

The management of the casino was divided into three departments, each under a separate chief. The *service intérieur* looked after the commissariat, general maintenance and the domestic and outside staff, but not the croupiers. The *service extérieur* concerned itself with public services – such as the new drainage project – and formed a link between the casino and the municipality. Lastly, and perhaps most importantly, the *directeur des jeux* was in charge of everything to do with the gaming rooms and play. His duties were more varied than the name suggests. His office was the nerve centre of the establishment. It was strategically situated behind the desk at which the admission tickets were issued, next to the gaming rooms and directly below the doctor's premises and surgery. All that separated him from the nearest roulette wheel was a small concealed door.

Without moving from his desk the director could hear if anything untoward broke the rhythm his ear was normally attuned to: the clink of the coins and the buzz of conversation and the regular punctuation of the croupiers' announcements. Should, for instance, a gambler – it had been known to happen – be seized with an attack of screaming or hysterical laughter, the surgery was close at hand; and if other attention was needed the director could be on the spot in a few seconds, ready for whatever action was necessary. But he was more often summoned from the side where the entrance tickets were issued. Undesirables could be identified through the personal files: and anyone on the black list was spotted and turned away. The noisy protests and ugly scenes this sometimes gave rise to also called for his intervention. These disputes were of a personal kind, to be settled only with patience and courtesy and tact. Rough stuff was mercifully rare, for there were no regular police on the premises. But casino officials known as *commissaires* were empowered to arrest people, conduct them to the door and hand them over to the authorities outside.

A criminal record was not the only grounds for exclusion. Monégasque subjects, residents of the principality and even inhabitants of the surrounding French département of the Alpes Maritimes were automatically debarred. Priests and officers in uniform and officers in civilian clothes from the neighbouring French and Italian garrisons came under the same ban. In this, the management's policy was really a protective one: on principle, they felt that no one should be let in who could not afford to lose the money in his pocket; but short of an inquisition into the circumstances of every player, the principle could hardly be applied and the existing rule was adopted as better than nothing. It did at least prevent any of the local population from ruining themselves.

Some people were excluded by a different clause. These were described as '*n'ayant pas de moyens*' and came under the heading of '*épuration*'. They were non-gamblers who aimlessly haunted the rooms long after their curiosity as mere onlookers must have been satisfied. Though not necessarily suspect – for there was no indication that they were loitering with intent – they added to the overcrowding and were politely weeded out. Another kind of excluded visitor was the *représentant de commerce*, from humble commercial travellers to the agents of big concerns. There was no personal objection to them; it was from fear that they might be tempted to gamble with their firms' money instead of their own. Since there could be no clear way of dividing the sheep from the goats, the *directeur des jeux* had to judge each case on its own merit and exercise his discretion.

His personnel steadily increased as extensions were added to the casino and by the turn of the century, when two more gaming rooms were opened at the height of the season, there were seventeen roulette and six trente-et-quarante tables in full swing. The running and supervision and the control of the crowds that gathered there called for a staff of over five hundred. Many were younger relatives of the men who had come from Homburg with François Blanc, but most of them were recruited locally and there was a preference for those who were already employed by the casino, usually in some other, more menial, capacity. Since the number of tables functioning varied with the season, some were part-time employees. Others were only engaged for four months in the year. Even for these posts there were more applicants than vacancies.

It was impossible to become a fully-fledged croupier overnight. The candidates had first to prove themselves 'thoroughly trustworthy, well behaved, obliging and courteous, tidy, clean in their habits, and simply but well dressed'. Then came six months' training at an evening school in the casino, which opened when the day's work was over. They learnt the art of spinning the wheel evenly with the forefinger and the middle finger, rolling the ball with only the thumb and forefinger, stacking the chips in exact units of twenty, placing bets for players, tossing the plaques or gold coins with such precision that they fell directly on the number indicated, paying off a successful gambler with a cascade of coins which landed straight in front of him, raking in the losing chips without disturbing the winning ones – no easy matter – memorizing the dozens of different bets by dozens of different gamblers and being able to multiply instantaneously the number of winning chips by thirty-five, seventeen, eleven or eight according to the type of bet from *carré* to *en plein*.

Considering the manual dexterity and the mathematical proficiency demanded, the croupiers were adequately but no lavishly paid. The highest salary was five hundred francs a month. Their daily spells of duty were alternately of five and six hours. At one time the management had raised no objection to their being given gratuities, but individual tipping had since been forbidden and now no croupier was allowed to accept anything for himself. The *sous-chef* alone was permitted to receive a present, and only on behalf of all the others employed at the table. The collective nature of the gift was implicit in the formula of thanks: *'Merci pour le personnel'*.* Social intercourse between the staff and the players was discouraged on the same principle; there was always the risk of swindlers trying to make friends with the croupiers in order to suborn them. The management feared that even honest and honourable kindness could lead to trouble. Croupiers were men of humble station and if they were invited by rich visitors to luxurious hotels or villas they might become dissatisfied with their lot and tempted to dishonesty.

Considering their pay and living conditions, it was astonishing how few of them proved to be dishonest. Every day of their lives, and several times a day, they saw, as one of them explained, a year's salary lost and won as easily as penny stakes on a game of cards at home. They raked in and handled hundreds and hundreds of gold coins after every turn of the wheel. Their dinner-jackets were made without pockets, but after their special training it would have been tempting to make a coin or two vanish by sleight of hand – by slipping them inside the collar under cover of neck-scratching, for instance – yet hardly any of them succumbed.

---

* Even then the money did not go entirely to the staff. Until 1948, when the croupiers staged a sit-down strike, the management took fifty per cent of the tips. Now it takes only thirty per cent.

10

THE
GOLDEN AGE

Monte Carlo was beginning its golden age, the period in its history which more or less coincided with the Edwardian Era in England and the Belle Epoque in France. Gambling had become accepted as a fashionable but legitimate pastime, an allowable recreation even for ladies of most exalted station. 'Sooner or later all the world is to be seen in the gaming rooms,' a young English debutante wrote home enthusiastically. 'At Monte Carlo I saw Lady Randolph Churchill in the height of her dark Southern beauty, lovely Miss Muriel Wilson, Mrs Langtry . . .'

She might have added the king of Sweden to her list and the king of Württemberg, the prince and princess of Braganza, the prince of Saxe-Meiningen, the prince of Serbia, Prince Mirza Riza Khan of Persia, the Aga Khan, the rajah of Pudukota, the prince of Denmark, the princess of Pless, Prince Hohenlohe, Prince Kotchoubey, Prince Radziwill, Grand Duke Serge of Russia, the grand duke of Luxembourg, Grand Duke Nicholas, Grand Duke Boris, the duchess of Roxburgh, the duke and duchess of Marlborough, the duke of Norfolk, the duke of Montrose, the duchess of Sutherland, Lord Victor Paget, Sir Hugo de Bathe, Sir Walter Ingram, Lord Wolverton, Lord Farquhar, Lord Cecil Manners . . . She could have ended with a handful of the American millionaires – Charles M. Schwab, Pierpont Morgan, W. K. Vanderbilt and James Gordon Bennett. The catalogue was interminable.

The Hôtel de Paris had become too small to hold these glittering figures and a magnificent new hotel called the Hermitage was opened in 1898. The two entirely separate wings stood two hundred yards apart. Until these were joined together ten years later by the grandly named Pavilion des Princes, carriages ferried the guests between their rooms and the restaurant. Here is a typical dinner:

Saumon Fumé de Hollande
Ox-tail Clair en Tasse
Velouté de Homard au Paprika
Truite Saumonée à la Chambord
Tourte de Ris-de-Veau Brillat-Savarin
Selle d'Agneau de Lait Polignac
Pommes Dauphin   Petits Pois Fine-Fleur
Caille de Vigne à la Richelieu
Sorbet au Clicquot
Poularde Soufflée Impériale
Pâté de Foie Gras d'Alsace
Salade Aïda
Asperges d'Argenteuil Sauce Mousseline
Buisson d'Ecrevisses à la Nage
Crêpes Flambées au Grand Marnier
Ananas Givré à l'Orientale
Coffret de Friandises
Corbeille de Fruits   Café   Liqueurs

Special trains carried all these fashionable visitors to the Riviera. They ran from the principal capitals of Europe, and the most luxurious was the St Petersburg–Vienna–Cannes express, which had card-rooms and writing-saloons in addition to a dining-car where the cooking was equal to that of the best restaurants in Paris. Passengers made a point of dressing for dinner.

Evening dress too – not merely a dinner-jacket, but tails and a white tie – was always worn at the Monte Carlo Sporting Club, but these sartorial standards did not apply in the casino itself.

Once, poorly dressed people had been kept out in the hopes of raising the tone of the rooms: Lord Salisbury, when he was actually Foreign Secretary, was refused admission for looking too shabby, and he was not at first believed when he said who he was. But now fashion experts set on record the most extraordinary mixture of clothes. Everything but knickerbockers was admitted ... and the people were equally mixed: respectable British matrons, harridans with systems, harlots from Paris. The presence there of so many rich and extravagant visitors drew *filles de joie* to Monte Carlo in convoys. During the season the famous Paris cocottes, who were usually seen at Maxim's, thronged the casinos. Their beauty roused the wonder of the newly wed young duchess of Marlborough, who asked her husband who they were. 'I was surprised,' she later wrote, 'by his evasive answers and still more startled when informed that I must not look at the women whose beauty I admired. It was only after repeated questioning that I learned that they were ladies of easy virtue ...'

The most spectacular were Liane de Pougy and La Belle Otero, both at the height of their beauty and glory. Liane, born Anne de Chassaigne, the daughter of a French army officer, was deferentially known as '*notre courtisane nationale*'. It was said that Caroline Otero, an Andalusian gypsy dancer, had slept in more royal beds than any other woman in Europe. They both gambled heavily and their rivalry was the subject of countless anecdotes.

One evening La Belle Otero decided to outdazzle her rival by entering the casino in an evening gown as low-cut as the law allowed and wearing her entire collection of jewellery, which included two pearl necklaces that had once belonged to the Empress Eugénie and the empress of Austria respectively, and a diamond bolero made for her by Cartier and valued at nearly three million francs. A few minutes later Liane, who had been forewarned of La Belle Otero's decision, made her own appearance wearing a white dress of classic simplicity and a single diamond drop at her throat, but followed by her maid carrying all her other jewels on a velvet cushion. This, like all anecdotes about Monte Carlo, must not be taken quite literally. According to a second version, the maid was not carrying the jewels but wearing them.

In a third version they were worn not by Otero's maid but by her dog – either a fox-terrier or a poodle; even on this point the version disagrees. Dogs were not allowed in the casino ... But then a fourth version claims that the incident did not happen in Monte Carlo at all but at Maxim's; while a fifth depicts Otero, in a *black* dress, turning the tables on Liane de Pougy.

It was Monte Carlo that had originally launched La Belle Otero. The child bride of an Italian nobleman who had gambled away his fortune, she is said to have restored it by staking two louis – all the money she had – on red at trente-et-quarante. She knew nothing of the game, and thinking she had lost, moved away. A few minutes later, she records, 'I happened to pass by the table where I had staked my two louis. I noticed an imposing pile of money ... Red had come up twenty-eight times running and my two louis had become fifty thousand francs.' (This story, too, must be taken with a grain of salt. Another version states that although she had never set eyes on a roulette wheel, she played four single winning numbers in turn and placed all the winnings back on the table each time and all but broke the bank.)

It was Monte Carlo that broke her, too. She retired in 1922 at the age of forty-five with capital reckoned at fifty million francs, but in a few years she had gambled it all away. Penniless, she moved into a one-room apartment in Nice, where she lived on a small allowance paid by the casino. She died there more than forty years later.

By the turn of the century over a million foreigners visited the principality every year. Not all of them came to gamble; there were many attractions besides the casino. Under the direction of Raoul Gunsbourg the Monte Carlo Opera had become the rival of Paris, Berlin, London and New York. Leading composers wrote especially for the opera there, notably Massenet; *Don Quichotte*, *Thérèse* and *Le Jongleur de Notre-Dame* all had their world premières at Monte Carlo. It was here, too, that the young Caruso experienced his first triumph when, in the spring of 1902, he sang in *La Bohème* with Melba; and Chaliapin, Gunsbourg's greatest discovery, first appeared at Monte Carlo in the following year, singing in Boito's *Mefistofele*. Like all the other famous performers engaged by the casino, he was paid larger fees than anywhere else but invariably gambled them away.

Pigeon-shooting was still a favourite pursuit in some circles and the place had a fresh burst of publicity in 1903, when the Grand Prix du Littoral was won by Tod Sloan. Six years earlier this American jockey had revolutionized English horse-racing with his introduction of the crouching seat; but he had lost his licence later. He had usually struck lucky at Monte Carlo. On his first visit he won over sixty thousand francs playing twice daily for six days. The year he won the shooting competition, he had been losing heavily; he had to borrow the two hundred francs for his entrance fee. But he backed himself at fifty to one with a second loan of two hundred francs, adding a further ten thousand to his ten thousand francs prize money, and he at once carried his winnings to the casino and made a hundred thousand francs more. He died penniless thirty years later.

In the last week of December 1903 the body of an Englishman called George Allender was found in a deserted ravine near the Corniche road. He had been robbed and then stabbed to death. The crime caused a sensation because, contrary to the belief that gambling led so often to crime that murders were bound to be frequent, there had been in fact only four local convictions for murder in the previous ten years. This fact may have been partly due to the proximity of the French frontier. Enemies of the casino used to assert that the Monégasque authorities conducted would-be murderers to the border, to make sure they committed their crime the other side. There was no reciprocity between the principality and France with regard to powers of arrest and a criminal could cross the border simply by stepping off the pavement of the Boulevard des Moulins into France. So it was easy for Camille Blanc to deny that the casino was in any way responsible for Allender's death. 'When there is a crime in Monte Carlo,' he said, 'come to me and I will see that justice is done. But I can't assume the functions of the President of the French Republic.'

A more sensational crime was committed in the principality four years later. Early in the morning of 6 August 1907 a trunk was deposited in the cloakroom of the Gare Saint-Charles in Marseilles and a few hours later it began to leak blood. The police were summoned and the trunk was found to contain the headless and legless body of a middle-aged woman. She was identified as Emma Liven, a Danish widow, last seen in the lounge of the Hôtel de Paris, and the trunk was traced back to a married couple who had registered as Mr and Mrs Jervis at the Hôtel du Louvre et de la Paix in the Canebière. They were arrested in possession of a valise containing the missing head and legs.

They confessed that their real name was Goold, and at first the man claimed to be Sir Vere Thomas St Leger Goold, Bt, the head of an old Irish family from County Cork. Later he admitted that he had no title; he was only the baronet's younger brother. His wife, Marie Violette, *neé* Girodin, was French and a year or two older. It was never established whether he was her third or her fourth husband – her matrimonial statistics were lost in the maze of her lies – and for the last month they had rented a flat in a Monte Carlo villa. Confronted with the mangled remains in their luggage, they could hardly deny knowing Emma Liven, but they rejected all responsibility for her death. After making various contradictory statements, they agreed on the following:

On the afternoon of 4 August, just after Madame Liven had called on Madame Goold at the Villa Milesimo, a young man of about thirty burst in and, addressing the Danish widow, said: 'Wretched woman, you have ruined me!' He then stabbed her with a knife. Madame Goold fainted and remembered no more. When she recovered, the young man had gone and Emma Liven was lying dead before her. She and her husband, who had meanwhile come home, dreading that they might be accused of the crime, cut up the body, placed part of it in the trunk and the remainder in the valise, and took train for Marseilles.

This story failed to convince the police. They continued to interrogate the two suspects until Mrs Goold at last broke down and confessed that her husband had committed the murder in a fit of drunkenness: coming downstairs, she had found him bending over his lifeless victim with a blood-stained dagger in his hand. Then he had cut up the body and stowed it away in the trunk; she herself had played no part in the grisly task.

Again the police were unconvinced, even when Goold corroborated his wife's statement. He affirmed that Madame Liven had angered him by asking for money and he had picked up a knife in a paroxysm of rage, stabbed her to death and cut up the body unaided. This confession would have been enough to send him to the guillotine, but somehow it did not ring true. He was a drunkard, and perhaps capable of murder in his cups, but that he could deliberately have planned such a crime was somehow unimaginable. When sober, he was a listless character entirely dominated by his wife, yet everything in this case pointed to premeditation. The Goolds were known to be hard up, and Mrs Liven might have been lured to the villa for the sake of her jewels. If this were so, Mrs Goold was the likelier suspect. But it still remained to be proved.

A few weeks later the Goolds were brought back to the actual spot in Monte Carlo and forced to attend a reconstruction of the crime. On seeing three detectives re-enact the deed *in situ*, Mrs Goold persevered in her denial and accusation; but Goold, as though in a daze, admitted the truth at last. Yes, his wife had invited Emma Liven to tea and brained her with a mallet, while he stabbed her in the back; they had cut up the body together.

Their trial took place in December and Mrs Goold was sentenced to death and her husband to life imprisonment. Her sentence was eventually commuted to life imprisonment, and both of them were sent to Devil's Island, where they died one after the other in a short space of time.

A serious threat arose in 1907 when the French government decided to revise its gambling laws and allow certain games of chance to be played in public. Roulette and trente-et-quarante were still forbidden, but now baccara was legalized for the first time since 1837, and plans were made to build casinos in various resorts along the coast, notably at Cannes and Nice. These were the first rivals which Monte Carlo had had to face since the abolition of the casino in Saxon-les-Bains in 1878, but for the time being the danger was only potential.

The threat aggravated the political unrest which had begun to simmer in the principality. For some time, and with some justification, the native Monégasques had been alarmed by the ever-increasing number of foreigners employed by the casino and in the government, while they themselves lived under a patriarchal system. They felt they should have some say in their own finances and administration, especially now that the risk of competition might lead in time to the abolition of the casino. Agitation came to a head in October 1910, when a hostile crowd gathered outside the palace and shouted for a constitution. Meanwhile, with the agreement of the prince, a contingent of British sailors from Villefranche arrived on leave. They had instructions to watch the flagstaff of the Hôtel de Paris, which, ostensibly, had just laid in a new stock of wine. If a flag were hoisted they were to move in and open the wine-cases and if necessary restore order – or at least protect British property – with the arms and ammunition they would find inside them. At the same time French troops were ordered to stand by at Villefranche and Menton ready to converge on Monaco at a moment's notice.

No serious disturbance occurred, but the prince was alarmed enough to grant his subjects a constitution. His own sovereignty was maintained, but the Monégasques were granted individual liberty, freedom of speech, the right to petition, freedom of religion and the freedom *not* to observe religious fête days! They were also granted universal suffrage, with the right to a national council of twenty-one members. Appointed for four years, they had the power to insist that the prince should promulgate any new law they desired; but since he was himself empowered to dissolve this council when he liked, this article of the constitution did not amount to very much.

These concessions came too late. The Monégasques had been nearly obliterated by the foreign invasion. In 1861 the population had numbered 1,200, nearly all of them native Monégasques. But as most of the women since then had married foreigners, their children were no longer Monégasques; and by 1908, out of a population of 19,121, there were only 1,482 Monégasques by birth or naturalization, of whom not more than 635 were real natives. Out of a total potential electorate of 448, most of the voters were naturalized Italians. Only ninety-five genuine, native-born Monégasques were entitled to the franchise. But better only ninety-five than none at all.

Economically, the casino continued to rule the roost. One and a half million foreigners visited Monte Carlo in 1909. Few of these were regular gamblers. A special check was kept to discover the exact number. The number, for a single year, was only 150,950 and they lost on an average about two hundred francs* each. The rooms, however, were crowded by more and more spectators, and further extensions were called for. The eastward expansion of the building had already spread as far as it could go on level ground. When it reached the edge of the cliff, the new gaming room – known as the Salle Empire – had to be built above a basement leaning on the slope in order to bring it level with the rest. This new wing, with the Salle Touzet, were now the *salles privées* where, in the hope of choking off the wrong public, an additional charge – fifty francs in 1911, one hundred in 1912 – was made for admission. The Salle Schmidt, where stakes were lower, hours shorter, and the public less smart, was disparagingly known as the 'kitchen'.

In 1912 there was a serious attempt to determine the frequency of suicides and to classify them. There were ten between 1 April and 31 December in 1910, five of them counted as gamblers. Up to 31 March next year, there were four more, all gamblers. Thus, out of the 184,000 persons who were admitted to the gaming rooms during this period, nine committed suicide – a death-rate equivalent to 0.049 per 1,000. But out of the 20,000 inhabitants who were denied entry to the gaming rooms, no fewer than four died by their own hands – a death-rate equivalent to 0.2 per 1,000: twice as high as the suicide death-rate of London.

This classification was only approximate. The suicide in January 1911 was that of a twenty-five-year-old Russian; in

* In other words £8 – equivalent, incidentally, to the average income tax paid in Great Britain at that time.

February of a middle-aged Austrian and his wife; in March of another Austrian, aged thirty-four: all due to gambling. But the lady's maid who committed suicide in April did not gamble: she had lent her savings to her mistress, who lost them at roulette. And there was a gardener, also a non-gambler, who threw himself off the Rock of Monaco: his wife, obsessed by the flashy smartness of the place, had been eternally complaining that she was not well enough dressed. And the suicide of a coachman a little later was the result of increasing competition from motor-cars. Several of his colleagues, fearing for their livelihood, had died by their own hands for the same reason.

Camille Blanc followed up his new bent of drawing non-gamblers by a growing array of lures which were wholly unconnected with the casino. In 1910 one of the earliest French pilots, called Henri Rougier, climbed into his little biplane and skimmed six hundred feet above the Tête de Chien and over the Bay of Monaco and then flew out to sea – such a display had never been attempted before. Next year Blanc launched the first Monte Carlo Rally, and Rougier came in first. He had scorched through the 960 kilometres from Paris in just over twenty-eight hours. In 1911, the world of Monte Carlo was dazzled and spellbound by the first appearance of the Russian Ballet. Diaghilev's *Shéhérazade* was followed by the first vision of Karsavina and Nijinsky dancing in Bakst's scenery for *Le Spectre de la Rose*.

One of Camille Blanc's most extravagant projects came into being with the opening of the Monte Carlo Golf Course in 1912. Mont Agel, a rocky height shooting up vertically behind the casino, was the only site available for the links. The toil had been enormous. Huge rocks had had to be blasted out and carted off, hundreds of tons of earth transported and laid and then sown with grass that could outlive the withering blaze of a Riviera summer. The cost – over six million francs, it was whispered – had been tremendous. But with the casino making nearly fifty million francs, the fame of the accomplishment was reward enough. Outside England there were only three other golf courses – at Mandelieu, Pau and near Paris – in the whole continent of Europe.

Aviation was still new and something of a wonder. The Schneider Trophy, which Blanc set going in 1913, gave it a great boost. The first time was a fiasco; a mistral blew hard during all the ten days before the race and most of the pioneer aircraft due to compete were irreparably damaged during the trials. Next year the second race for the Schneider Trophy followed a general flying rally and the cup was won by an Englishman called Howard Pixton, who broke the world speed record at 92.1 miles an hour in a Sopwith seaplane.

Laurels crowned the achievements of Camille Blanc when the prince invested him in 1913 with the ribbon and star of a Grand Officer of the Order of Saint-Charles. It was his last triumph. War was imminent. Monte Carlo teemed with German generals and Italian royalty; intrigue abounded. It was even rumoured that some Italian officers had dressed themselves up as workmen to spy out the fortress of Mont Agel . . . On 4 August 1914 the prince proclaimed Monaco's neutrality, and the casino was closed for the second time since its foundation.

11

SLUMP
AND BOOM

The outbreak of war smote the little principality with a helpless inertia. Uncertainty reigned. Gambling ceased as suddenly, someone said, 'as if death had struck the croupiers in the very act of spinning the little white ball'.

There seemed little hope of the casino reopening that season. Out of a staff of eight hundred nearly three hundred were called to the colours in France and the rest were kept on by the company on reduced salaries. The gaming rooms were deserted, green baize covers discreetly shrouded the tables and the atrium was put at the disposal of the Red Cross. In spite of war, Camille Blanc still trusted in the arrival of old clients from Russia and South America and the United States. Otherwise the local economy was bound to suffer; in a measure the whole region depended on it. He knew that business would be slight until the Germans were driven out of France. But he sank half a million francs in publicity and reopened the Sporting Club in mid-November and the casino itself on 1 January 1915.

Although the profits plunged from thirty-six million francs a year to just over twelve million, somehow the casino kept going through the war. As a state that on paper was neutral – an enclave within France, close to the Italian border and with a Mediterranean harbour – Monte Carlo bubbled with intrigue and espionage. Secret agents flocked in from London and Paris and Berlin and Moscow, and though uniform was still forbidden the casino was thronged every night with rival intelligence officers in civilian clothes.

Many of its members had been called up, but the casino orchestra played on and Blanc did his best to keep going entertainment, in spite of restrictions. In 1916 he engaged the services of the popular 'oriental' dancer, Mata Hari. She was pursued with ardour by a handsome Russian colonel on leave in Monte Carlo. After the show one evening he went up and embraced her and kissed her passionately on the lips. Drawing a small pistol from her bosom, she shot him in the chest. The wound was slight; she was 'defending her honour'; it was hushed up. But she was asked to leave and drove away towards Spain in a big white Hispano-Suiza, and the unexplained incident seemed to be closed.

The truth emerged at her trial the following year. The Russian colonel was an Allied agent with orders to find out whether or not she was a spy. Information was leaked to the Germans that he was in possession of some vitally important papers. Posing as an admirer, he had entertained her in his villa and left his desk unlocked while he went out for a moment. The planted papers duly vanished, and the dancer left for her evening performance. In the hopes of catching her with the evidence (instead of reporting to his superiors) he had pretended to be drunk and seized her, and had almost paid with his life. But the Deuxième Bureau kept her under close watch and soon came upon further proof. She was executed by a firing squad on 15 October 1917.

The casino stayed open, but the principality was in low water. When Prince Albert asked Camille Blanc for an advance on his post-war takings, he was refused on the grounds that business was so poor. He approached Sir Basil Zaharoff, and the Levantine armaments magnate handed over twenty-five million francs on the understanding that it should be kept secret and that he would take control of the casino on a future date of his own choosing.

Zaharoff had been coming to Monte Carlo for thirty years; he stayed a few weeks every winter at the Hôtel de Paris with his Spanish mistress, the Duquesa de Marquena y Villafranca. But he had shown no interest in the casino and had never set foot in the gaming rooms. It could not have been the company's relatively small profits that prompted his decision: he was a multi-millionaire. The casino's security files, described as a world-wide rogues' gallery, could have tempted him earlier. But he had reached the height of his power and such instruments had lost their value. The answer may be found in another secret agreement, this time between the prince and Clemenceau, which confirmed the sovereignty of Monaco and pledged France to come to the rescue if the casino failed. It seems strange that a French prime minister should sign away a territory which, for all its seeming independence, was virtually a province of France. But, unlike most of his compatriots, Clemenceau was on friendly terms with Zaharoff; and to Zaharoff the independence of Monaco was crucial. For his real purpose in backing the prince was to take over not only the company but the principality itself. His secret aim was to oust the Grimaldis and bestow the throne on his mistress as soon as she was free to become his wife. Her husband was still alive, but insane and in an asylum.

One other obstacle remained. Prince Albert was nearly seventy and his son Prince Louis was a bachelor. The Grimaldi line was in danger of extinction. There were rumours already of French annexation impending; indeed, a secret clause laid down that Monaco would fall under French protection in default of an heir. Zaharoff had to prevent this. On 7 November a new bill entitled Prince Louis, succession failing, to nominate an heir; and the prompt adoption of his illegitimate daughter Charlotte assured the continuance of the Grimaldi line. Zaharoff could put his scheme into effect.

Prince Albert blamed Camille Blanc for the drop in the casino's takings, and a campaign was now launched to oust him. Signs of mismanagement were not lacking. Even when the revenue had risen after the war, the profits were nearly wiped out by the expenses: in 1920 they soared to forty million francs. The prince subjected the company to an audit: the number of employees had swollen to an army three thousand strong and the chief officials were receiving exorbitant salaries. Zaharoff's agents began stealthily buying shares until he owned the majority. But he let his option rest until the spring of 1923, when he learnt that his mistress's husband was dying. He arrived in Monte Carlo, called a special meeting and informed the board of his intention of taking control. Camille Blanc had to resign, 'for reasons of health' – he died five years later – and René Léon, one of Zaharoff's associates, was appointed administrator.

But the mad Spanish duke, though on his deathbed, still remained alive. Zaharoff had to bide his time. His first concern was to put the company on a profitable basis, and he set about it with characteristic ruthlessness. Gone the paternalism of the Blanc régime! The new directorate turned the casino into a prosaic business concern. For the first time an admission fee was charged for the 'kitchen'. 'If people will insist on losing their money,' said Zaharoff, 'they must pay for the privilege.' The pensions which Camille Blanc had granted to several hundred *décavés* were replaced by a cash settlement equivalent to two months' income and a one-way ticket to Paris. Many a ruined gambler, recognizing Zaharoff at his favourite table on the terrace of the Hôtel de Paris, mustered the courage to go up to him and plead: 'Sir Basil, I have lost all my money. You are the richest man in the world . . .' No one ever got further; he was cut short with a surly, 'Go to the devil!' When an English lady approached him – 'Help me, Sir Basil! Everything here belongs to you. You must know how to win.' – he deigned to reply: 'I can tell you how not to lose.' 'Oh, please!' she begged. 'Don't play,' he curtly told her.

Within a few weeks of his taking over, the casino began to prosper. Revenue rose to a hundred million francs and expenditure was reduced by a million. Further good news followed: a cable from Spain announced the death of the duke. On 22 September 1924, at the age of seventy-five, Zaharoff married the woman he had been in love with for nearly forty years. The time had come for his bid for the throne.

When Prince Albert died in 1922, he was succeeded by his son. Feelers as to the possibility of the new prince's selling out were firmly rejected, and shortly afterwards *L'Impartial*, a newly established Nice paper, launched a series of attacks accusing Prince Louis of dishonesty and extravagance, raking up his youthful dissipations and calling for his abdication. These were promptly countered by *Tout Va*, a new Monaco weekly. The editor, Sylvan Fabi, revealed that *L'Impartial* was financed by Zaharoff and the source of the slanders was left in no doubt. 'The principality,' wrote Fabi, 'knows only one head: His Most Serene Highness, Prince Louis II, and the others, whether they call themselves Zaharoff or René Léon, are nothing but casino creatures.'

The counter-attack was vigorously kept up. Another editorial described Zaharoff as *le métèque de la finance internationale* and went on to say: '. . . typical of the scoundrels who make bold to attack the prince, spit on his honour, aim at his throne! Their manoeuvres are condemned to failure, but what do they hide? Monsieur Zaharoff aspires to rule Monaco . . . Yet Prince Louis' sovereignty is upheld by the League of Nations, a power none shall challenge with impunity!'

The newspaper duel went on all through the year. Zaharoff showed no signs of slackening his efforts to unseat the prince and Fabi's editorials grew more outspoken and shrill: 'Just because he has managed to grab most of the shares, this disgusting and insatiable tyrant with his court of golden-calf-worshipping lackeys thinks he owns the country . . .'

But next year Zaharoff's campaign abruptly ceased. The following announcement appeared in the obituary column of *Le Temps*: 'Yesterday, after a short illness, in Monte Carlo, Madame Basil Zaharoff, Duchess of Villafranca.'

With her death, Zaharoff's princely ambitions collapsed. He had no further interest in the throne of Monaco and no further use for the casino. A few weeks later he sold his interests to the Paris banking house of Daniel Dreyfus. Shareholders in the company may have regretted his departure – their last dividend had reached a record one hundred per cent – but he himself had no cause for regret: he sold out for three times more than he had paid. The disgruntled and disappointed old autocrat lingered on at the Hôtel de Paris and died there ten years later.

It was the beginning of a new epoch in Monte Carlo's history. As an old gambler himself, the new administrator, René Léon, was able to run the casino with an outlook that was different from that of a glorified croupier. One evening shortly before his appointment, when he and his friend General Polovtsoff were about to leave after losing all their ready cash, he trod on a twenty-franc chip that somebody had dropped. Though he knew – who better? – that anyone who picked up a stray chip was liable to expulsion from the casino, he took the risk and, at the general's suggestion, put the twenty francs *à cheval* on 26–29. 29 duly obliged, and came up twice more within half a dozen spins of the wheel.

'Now let's go,' said the general, determined to leave before their luck turned.

'Just a moment,' Léon replied. 'There's something we mustn't forget.' And with an exaggeratedly straight face he handed the original chip to the *chef de partie* as though he had just found it.

One of his first moves after taking over the casino was to appoint his friend to the post of president of the Sporting Club – a poetically just choice, for the general was the son of a rich Russian who had lost millions of francs at the tables and had subsequently been ruined by the Revolution. The event had had a direct effect on Monte Carlo: most of the Russian grand dukes and a whole galaxy of Russian aristocrats, Europe's heaviest gamblers, had suddenly vanished from the scene. The eclipse of the German and Austro–Hungarian empires had wiped out another steady source of income. For a short time after the armistice the dollars of the freshly minted American millionaires were some kind of a stand-in for the former riches of the Central European aristocracy, but the flow was gradually diverted to the newer casinos in Nice and Cannes.

Since the role of the cocotte was now usurped by amateurs from the Almanach de Gotha, Debrett's and the Social Register, Monte Carlo had also been abandoned by the rich roués of yesteryear. There was so much promiscuity in European and American society that it was no longer necessary to travel all the way to the Riviera. It had been chiefly a winter resort for rich people in flight from a bad home climate and able to settle there for weeks or months. It was now in danger of being neglected completely in favour of the newly discovered Antibes, Cap Ferrat and Juan-les-Pins, which though less fashionable were far cheaper and more informal, and therefore more popular. René Léon realized that if it was to survive and compete with such places as these, he would have to create what neither François Blanc nor his son had ever contemplated: a summer season.

Cruises from America already dropped anchor at Monaco and in 1922 the Cunard liner *Cameronia* created a precedent by landing eight hundred visitors in the Bay of Hercules in mid-July. In spite of its name the Société des Bains de Mer had never done anything about sea-bathing. The Thermes Valentia of 1912 were merely a replacement of the old health baths of François Blanc's day. Monaco's coast was rocky for bathers: there was no beach to bask on. This lack had struck Elsa Maxwell when she called on her friend, the opera singer Mary Gordon, who was considered most eccentric for staying in the Hôtel du Parc in the summer. It was almost deserted, and so were all the others. The only amusement was to hire a boat and go out fishing.

In Venice Miss Maxwell had contrived to turn the Lido from a family beach for middle-class Italians into a smart international meeting-place. Prince Pierre de Polignac, Prince Louis's son-in-law, asked her to perform a similar act of transformation for Monte Carlo. She joined the management of the company on a two-year contract at ten thousand dollars' salary which she regularly lost at the tables.

Her first idea was to cover a pebbly beach with huge sheets of rubber and cover them with sand. She did not know, until tests proved it, that rubber soon perishes in sea water. A big blue-tiled swimming-pool was built instead. A Hollywood-style hotel in pink stucco was built behind the pool, to the design of the American architect Addison Mizner, and a new casino, handy for future inmates, went up two hundred yards away. A sliding roof made this white and gleaming structure the first place in the world where roulette could be played under the open sky. Grace Moore sang at the splendid opening in July 1927, and King Gustav of Sweden headed the guests.

Soon after, the opening was endorsed by a miracle! A 100-franc chip, seemingly flung from heaven, landed on number 8 at one of the roulette tables, just as the croupier announced '*Rien ne va plus.*' A diner in the restaurant above said he had dropped it by mistake; meanwhile number 8 had turned up and the croupier insisted on paying the inadvertent winner three thousand six hundred francs. Some say it was Yvonne Printemps who dropped the chip; others that Princess Faucigny-Lucinge, after a heavy loss and forgetting the tables below, had flung it fretfully away.

There were a few minor dramas that year. An Austrian woman was caught trying to change nineteen counterfeit 100-franc chips. She got fifteen months. A large number of these chips – but never the manufacturers – were discovered in another visitor's luggage. A few weeks later, in the early hours of 25 July, a young Jugoslav, who had been gambling daily for some time, suddenly whisked a bottle of petrol from his pocket, poured it over the table and tried to set it alight. Surrounded by a posse of casino officials, he drew an automatic and fired seven shots, hitting nobody but breaking several mirrors and candelabra. He tried to make a break for it, leapt from the window and fell into the garden and broke a leg. At the hospital his condition was not thought to be serious, but he died of heart failure that afternoon.

The event of the next year was the completion of the Country Club. It was one of René Léon's most ambitious schemes and designed to knock Cannes out of the saddle as the sports centre of the Riviera. It cost over twelve million francs and consisted of three enormous terraces for tennis courts which rested on walls of granite and descended in giant steps almost to the level of the sea, like the hanging gardens of Babylon, each of which was divided from the others by trellises of rambler roses. The clubhouse was long and one-storeyed and in the Moorish style, and shielded from the wind by sweeps of myrtle and cypress. The duke of Connaught gravely pronounced the club open, tossing a ceremonial tennis ball on to the centre court.

In February 1929 a new tide of counterfeit chips began to wash the tables, this time on such a scale that the design had to be changed at once. Again the source remained a mystery, but the forged admission tickets being sold a month later at the entrance desk were discovered to have been deftly forged by the officials themselves. These worries were nothing compared to the trouble which had sprung up between the casino and the Monaco communal council. A minor and quickly superseded dispute about sanitary conditions had developed into a constitutional crisis that involved the sovereign. He was hissed in public; and on 29 March five or six thousand people forced their way into the palace, calling for the dismissal of some of his dependants and even for his own deposition.

The old grievance about the employment of foreigners instead of Monégasques had plenty of substance to it. Only a quarter of the five hundred or so croupiers were Monégasques: the directors, the chief officials and most of the shareholders were French. Geography – this rocky enclave in France was entirely dependent for its economy on foreign favour and custom – was largely to blame, and an added cause lay in the paradox of the population. Out of twenty-five thousand inhabitants, some ten thousand were Italians and nine thousand were French; only 1,574 were listed as Monégasques within the strict meaning of the word. There were actually 668 more English residents than Monégasques. The remainder included a few hundred Americans, Swiss and Russians, and little groups of Dutch, Hungarians, Czechoslovaks, Germans, Jugoslavs, Turks, Greeks, and even Persians. In spite of the slight Italian preponderance, the state institutions – the postal, railway, customs and telegraphic services – were all French.

About the growing clamour for more democratic constitutional privileges which backed the foreign labour complaints, the prince tried to compromise. But he was in an awkward position. Under the watchful gaze of shareholders and hotel-keepers, he was quite unable to apply French liberal democracy within his own dominion. On the other hand, Monégasques enjoyed privileges which were closed to the French. There was no conscription, no tax-collector knocking on the door. There might be occasional local water shortages or electric light failures; the gas might sometimes burn fitfully in the shops and cafés; but, covered as they were by the casino's yearly subsidy, they cost a fraction of the French public services just across the street. By now the contribution from the profits of the casino to public works and the running of the state was enormous. Other cash payments included the cost of a printing works and the upkeep of an official newspaper. The company also had to hand over fifty per cent of the takings of the tobacco monopoly and go surety for two thirds of the postal services and for two hundred and eighty thousand francs to cover each of the eighteen operatic performances given every season under the prince's patronage. To fulfil all these duties the company employed a staff of 3,800: a staff twice as large as the entire Monégasque population.

The prince settled matters for the time being by granting most of the demands of his subjects and promising reforms; all much to the dismay of René Léon and his associates, who regarded these pledges as the thin end of a fatal wedge: if the Monégasques got control of the state institutions they might ask for control of the casino itself, and they now seemed bent on winning legislative rights which could bring this about. Alternatively, under the pressure of changing times and on the pretext of *force majeure*, the prince might declare the concession null and void. Either contingency was alarming.

These fears were justified. In spite of the prince's pledges, trouble broke out again later, this time ostensibly over Léon's extravagant development programme. But it seemed rather late in the day to agitate against the cost of buildings that had been completed for several years, especially since, despite this outlay, the company had made gigantic profits – ninety-eight million francs in 1928, seventy-two million in 1929* – which had showered benefits on the state. Whatever the real motive, the outcry against the casino and the palace became so violent that on 26 December 1930 Prince Louis suspended the constitution by decree.

Léon followed Camille Blanc's example of multiplying the lures at Monte Carlo. The American chorus girls at the Summer Casino shed a new glamour and the Monte Carlo Grand Prix – the world's first round-the-houses motor-car race – provided a fresh range of thrills. And, in spite of the world economic crisis, the International

* By this time the value of the franc had been stabilized at 124.21 to the pound sterling.

Sporting Club – a huge white brand-new structure with gaming rooms, restaurant, ballroom, bar and a nightclub – was finished in 1932 for a fabulous but undisclosed sum. But profits for the year of the Great Slump dropped to thirty-two million francs and for the first time since the foundation no dividend was paid to the share-holders. In 1933 they dropped to sixteen million francs, but the new Sporting Club had proved a great success and the cost of all the outlay was nearly covered. The company managed to pay a dividend, and by June the situation in Monaco was stable enough for a return to constitutional government.

The decision of the French government to legalize roulette and trente-et-quarante was a grievous blow: hitherto Monte Carlo had had a monopoly of both games. It was now in competition with any French casino with sufficient financial reserves to withstand a run against the bank. On 22 December the roulette wheel spun for the first time at Cannes: although the day was a Friday and the first winning number to turn up was 13, it was the beginning of a successful career. Other casinos followed and Monte Carlo found itself at grips with Nice, Biarritz, Le Touquet and Deauville, and soon, since Italy refused to be left in the cold, with the Lido at Venice and with San Remo just across the border.

Thanks to Léon's foresight and pertinacity Monte Carlo suffered less from the slump than its rivals. The Sporting Club was the most fashionable rendezvous on the whole of the Riviera. The Monte Carlo Grand Prix continued to be a unique attraction, and the Rally was still the most popular long-distance motoring event in Europe. The country club was a favourite haunt of the king of Sweden; the Pasha of Marrakesh strode across the golf course at Mont Agel; Ronald Colman and William Powell cavorted in the swimming-pool of the Beach Hotel, and the Summer Casino seethed with crowned heads, film stars, dashing aristocrats and millionaires. The main casino stayed open all summer, but for a very different class of visitor, as a social annalist observed: youths in singlets, jaunty negresses, blowzy blondes in pink pyjamas, Spaniards with their jackets over their shoulders and sleeves loose, girls with raffia-coloured hair, middle-aged women in black, carry-ing their gambling systems under one arm, girls in green flannel trousers, and English couples in khaki breeches and old gentlemen in steaming braces.

On 5 February 1934 Léon broke new ground by providing a table at the Sporting Club with gold coins instead of the usual chips and plaques. The French mint was late in delivering the order he had given for eighteen-carat counters, so he bought up every American gold dollar piece he could get hold of in France and England. They came in denominations of twenty, ten and five, and five was the minimum stake. Gold had not been seen at the tables since before the war; its reintroduction, even on such a limited scale, was a triumphant success, but as most of the winners took their gold away with them instead of changing it back, the stock was exhausted in a few months and artificial money regained its sway.

It was the first year, too, of a new game played with three dice called Monte Carlo Hazard – *brelan* in French – but although a lucky gambler could win as much as 1,800 to 1 on a single throw, it never really caught on and in five years it was dead. In the summer Léon resigned for reasons of health. His resignation heralded a serious financial setback for the company. Receipts dropped badly and for the first time in its history the company published a balance sheet showing a loss. Since it was in the red to the tune of over six million francs, no dividend was paid to the shareholders in 1936, and the value of the shares plummeted.

At this time the Société des Bains de Mer was paying no less than seventy-three per cent of its receipts to the Monaco government. The cost of providing gas for the whole principality was nearly four million francs a year; the annual bill for electricity was nearly two million; and the water supply, sanitation, upkeep of roads, maintenance of the fire brigade and post office accounted for further vast sums which the company, in its present situation, could no longer afford. Henceforth, therefore, these public services were taken over by the government, which was compensated by an extra percentage on all casino takings in excess of thirty-five million francs; but even so a loan had to be raised for the company to carry on, and the staff was asked to take a cut in their salaries. As a result of these measures, and also because of a marked increase in the number of visitors – 257,000, the largest influx since 1926 – the balance sheet for the following year showed a profit of over two million francs, and the gross receipts were almost sixty million. And for 1938, despite the Munich crisis, the corresponding figures were no less than eight million and one hundred and eight million.

On the outbreak of war in September 1939 Prince Louis followed the example his father had set in August 1914 and declared Monaco a neutral sovereign state. As before, the staff of the SBM was so depleted by the mobilization of the French army that the summer Sporting Club was closed at once. The main casino, after continuing for a short time as best it could, was in its turn closed down. But the directors understood that if it remained closed indefinitely, not only the six hundred remaining employees would suffer but the local population as well. They therefore asked the staff to accept a cut in their salaries, as they had in 1935, and they managed to reopen the casino within three months. It was temporarily closed again when Italy entered the war. Despite Monaco's proclaimed neutrality, a contingent of Carabinieri invaded the principality and the company's 1940 balance sheet showed a loss of over five million francs. But after the fall of France and the influx into the principality of rich Jews and other refugees, the casino made a profit of six million. In 1942 the corresponding figure soared to twenty-eight million, then, in 1943 and again in 1944, to the record sum of one hundred and six million.

When the Allies landed in North Africa, the Germans spread throughout unoccupied France, and when they reached the Riviera they in their turn invaded the principality. The Hôtel de Paris was occupied first by the Gestapo, then by the headquarters staff of a Panzer division commanded by General von Kohlermann. Two batteries of defence troops installed gun emplacements, minefields and barbed-wire entanglements all along the coast. German officers patronized the casino, complying correctly with the regulations by wearing civilian clothes. So, unbeknown to them, did a British officer, Squadron-Leader Whitney Straight, likewise in plain clothes, having escaped from the prison camp at La Turbie.

The Germans enforced a blackout in Monaco where the Italians had failed, and they made sure that it was observed by sending up a small training aircraft every night which dropped hand-grenades and small bombs on any light that showed. But on von Kohlermann's orders the plane steered clear of the casino to avoid its being hit by accident. The building was badly shaken, however, when in the course of a successful attack on German shipping in Monte Carlo harbour two torpedoes fired from a British submarine exploded just below the *tir aux pigeons*. In the autumn of 1943 von Kohlermann once again helped to save the casino when he rejected the Gestapo's suggestion that the heavy copper roof should be removed and sent back to a Fatherland desperately short by then of any kind of metal. He declared it a cultural and historical monument.

Ironically the casino was in greater danger of destruction after the Allied landing on 15 August 1944 than during the whole of the enemy occupation. The American troops made no attempt to advance east of Nice; they drove straight up the Rhône Valley and their aircraft bombed Monte Carlo in an attempt to sink a German vessel in the harbour. One bomb scored a direct hit on the thermal establishment only four hundred yards from the casino. The German artillery in the fortress of Mont Agel was another hazard. Even after von Kohlermann's division pulled out at the end of the month, the artillerymen remained and fired at all vessels approaching the coast. Fortunately for the casino, none of their shells fell short.

American contingents eventually made their way along the coast, and on 3 September one of them reached Monte Carlo. Many of the officers and men had patronized the casino before the war. They were given a warm welcome, but even they were not allowed to enter the premises in uniform; they had to get some civilian clothes together before being admitted and, for this special occasion, the rooms were kept open until four in the morning. They only stayed a week. There was disagreement with the Monégasque government as to how many troops could be accommodated if Monte Carlo was made into a leave centre. The American authorities suggested twelve thousand; the government was unwilling to accept more than twelve hundred; and the principality was put out of bounds to all American and Allied troops.

Millions of francs and several months were needed to make good the wear and tear of the war. The Hôtel de Paris alone needed eight thousand metres of new carpeting. But by the end of 1945 Monte Carlo had more or less recovered its pre-war aspect. It was two years later that the rest of the heavily bombarded and harshly occupied Riviera lost the seedy and dilapidated look of an abandoned playground.

12

THE
NEW LOOK

The general downhill trend of world economy was marked in
Monte Carlo by a rare but significant event. In 1948 the croupiers
went on strike till they got seventy per cent of the tips instead of
the fifty the management allotted them. Wages and overheads rose,
receipts dwindled, currency restrictions cut down the spending of
rich English visitors; the Iron Curtain had sealed off the ex-
propriated ghosts of thousands of lavish and reckless clients; and
large-scale American gamblers were limited to a handful of
millionaires.

'Nine the field, ten is the point! . . . Same shooter coming out!
. . . Eight the easy way! . . .' These alien incantations started going
up in the Salle Schmidt in 1949, when the game of craps was
introduced in the hope of encouraging more tourists from the
United States. One-armed bandits were set up in the lobby at the
same time. Though everyone took to them, fruit machines didn't
pay at first; the resulting gains were as low as forty million heavily
devalued francs.*

As though to blazon forth Monte Carlo's decline, the rest of the
Riviera was booming. 'Monaco looks on the point of death,' said
an American observer. 'It is a slowly expiring community of
retired generals, drab gamblers and stray cats.' Yet only twenty
minutes away along the Lower Corniche, he found Nice a 'torrent

---

* At this time the value of the franc was pegged at 980 to the pound sterling
and 350 to the US dollar.

of life', with both casinos packed. Cannes was roaring ahead, and so was Juan-les-Pins. The visitors to Monte Carlo dropped to a quarter, and the casino takings to a tenth of the pre-war figures, and by 1951 the company was again running at a loss.

It was at this juncture that a *deus ex machina* appeared in the person of Aristotle Onassis. He had first caught sight of Monte Carlo from the sea on 21 September 1923, travelling steerage to seek his fortune in the New World on a crowded ship bound for Buenos Aires. His native town of Smyrna had been sacked by the Turks, and his family ruined. 'Every time I see the lights of Monte Carlo,' he remarked in later life, 'I think how beautiful they looked that night as we passed – to me and to a thousand other seasick and homesick exiles . . .'

Thirty years later Monte Carlo began to call him back. Midway between the two great ports of Genoa and Marseilles, it was a perfect base for a ship owner, and it was tax-free. 'If we have flags of convenience,' said Onassis, 'why not convenience headquarters too?' The old Sporting Club stood closed and empty; it was ideal for his purpose. He was well aware of the company's precarious finances, so he made an offer, but to his amazement it was refused. To reinforce his bid he bought a small packet of the company's shares; thanks to the casino's meagre prospects they were not hard to come by. Then he went on buying until, by 1954, he had amassed enough to give him control of the company and its properties, including the old Sporting Club, which was all he had wanted.

The word 'Onassis' was enough to revive the world's interest in the dying resort. Reports of his entertaining glamorous guests such as Greta Garbo at the Hôtel de Paris encouraged emulation in other celebrities. Mimetic luminaries of the International Set began herding to Monte Carlo in his wake. The 1955 New Year's party at the Hôtel de Paris was a complete sellout. Over a thousand people paid an average of forty thousand francs each, and for the first time in four years the company showed a profit.

Like Zaharoff, Onassis preferred hazarding vast sums on commercial ventures rather than gambling petty stakes at the tables, but he naturally wished to make the most of his investment and to put the company on its feet. His first action – a reorganization of the management – could only be carried through in conjunction with the reigning prince. During the difficult pre-war decade there had been no majority shareholder and Prince Louis had been given increased power in the appointment of officials. The president, directors and managers were all subject to his veto, and irrespective of the shareholders' wishes no appointment was valid if he chose to wield it. His grandson, Rainier, had inherited this right, and for all his wealth Onassis was obliged to comply. Prince Rainier, who was born on 31 May 1923, was the son of Prince Louis' daughter, Princess Charlotte, and of Prince Pierre de Polignac, who had assumed the name of Grimaldi by Sovereign Ordinance on 18 March 1920. He succeeded to the throne on his grandfather's death in 1949. Pierre Rey, the comptroller of the prince's household, was appointed president; Charles Simon, nominated by Onassis, was managing director.

Monte Carlo was in the news again. It remained to replace it on the map. Onassis devised projects as outrageous as Elsa Maxwell's and as ambitious as René Léon's, but before they could be put through a new crisis struck the principality. In the summer of 1955 Monaco's biggest bank, the Société Monégasque de Banques et de Métaux Précieux, went bankrupt.

Fortunately things turned out to be less serious than was originally feared. An interim inquiry showed that the deficit – about seven hundred million francs – might be reduced by a more exact valuation of its assets. But what had started as a financial issue soon assumed a political aspect. Prince Rainier himself became involved and several members of his household had to resign. Pierre Rey, however, remained in office as president of the company and the sum of four hundred and twenty million francs was found to have been suddenly and mysteriously entered in the credit column of the bank's books as 'anonymous loans'. All this gave rise to the rumour that Onassis was involved, though he declared that neither he nor the company had any connection with the bank. Rumour and denial both added to the enshrouding mystery, but there were no repercussions and the casino flourished.

The crap tables in the Salle Schmidt had become one of the

chief springs of revenue, and the brand-new type of crooked gambler they attracted was known as the 'dice-switcher'. In tough American 'sawdust joints' players had to roll up their sleeves, but the dice used here were green ones, made specially by a firm in Reno and considered impossible to counterfeit; and in any case vigilance would have made the theft of a genuine model extremely difficult. So the inspector on duty on 21 February 1956 had no grounds for suspicion when an American called Jason Lee started an astonishing run of luck by throwing winning combinations time after time. But it was noticed that he only staked small sums while a couple of other Americans had soon won over three million francs by betting on him heavily. The inspector picked up the dice Lee had been using and handed him a new pair. The two big winners made themselves scarce; and Lee, having lost his turn, likewise slipped away. His dice were found to be a slightly darker green than the official casino pieces, one millimetre smaller, two milligrams heavier, and so loaded that the winning combinations of 6 and 1, or 3 and 4, were bound to turn up at every throw.

The three crooks were arrested at Nice airport on the point of flying to Tangier, and their luggage yielded up nearly two hundred dice, some of them loaded to produce only winning sevens, while others had certain numbers missing. In spite of the *brigade de surveillance*, they had been copied from a pair previously lifted by Lee and skilfully copied. He and his two associates, who were called Arif Shaker and Philip Aggie, were sent back to Monaco for trial, convicted and imprisoned.

Thanks to Onassis, the lost fame of Monte Carlo had returned almost overnight. On 19 April 1956 it was lifted still higher by Prince Rainier's marriage to Grace Kelly. An unprecedented horde of journalists two thousand strong descended upon the principality. Publicity ran wild and the tide of visitors poured in and kept mounting year by year until it reached the peak of 650,000 in 1958 and the casino's turnover rose from one billion to two and a half billion francs.

The summer season – from mid-July to mid-September –

brought in almost as much now as the winter season between Christmas and Easter, thanks to the changes that had taken place under the Onassis dispensation. Not all of his schemes were successful. He made a bathing beach by covering the rocks with concrete and spreading sand on it, but it had to be abandoned when the sand was promptly washed away by the breakers. But everything owned by the company was renovated and redecorated. The Hôtel de Paris was enlarged at vast cost by the addition of four new floors and a penthouse grill room with a sliding roof. Work started on a tunnel and a new railway station and plans were made for reclaiming the land by the old Summer Sporting Club and building a sort of garden city. All these schemes, which were designed to benefit the government as well as the company, led to increasing friction between the prince and Onassis. At first it was thought that the management might be at fault, but the real trouble lay in the conflicting views of the two chief figures. The prince thought Onassis regarded Monte Carlo as merely another field for speculation; to Onassis the prince was biased in favour of his government to the detriment of the Société des Bains de Mer.

The first serious clash occurred when some buildings put up on the land reclaimed at the company's expense were almost immediately razed on the prince's orders to make way for a public bathing beach. It disinclined Onassis for similar ventures. Moreover, he had additional and more personal worries. In November his wife Tina filed a suit for divorce against him and within a few weeks there was a mysterious movement in SBM stock on the Paris Bourse. The shares, which had been worth about two thousand francs when Onassis first started buying them, had risen since to just under three thousand; now they jumped to almost five thousand francs. The only explanation seemed to be that Onassis was increasing his holding in order to tighten his control of the company: it was known that he needed only 20,001 more shares to give him an absolute majority. But at a press conference held at the Hôtel de Paris in mid-December he denied having bought any additional SBM stock in the past five months. He admitted, however, that 'a company in which he was interested' had for several months held more than half a million shares. In other words, he already had the absolute majority he wanted.

He did not divulge how this had come about, but there were rumours that his wife's father, the shipping magnate Stavros Livanos, was indirectly responsible. The movement on the Paris Bourse had apparently been caused by his attempting to compete with his son-in-law for control of the casino, but on this occasion – for the time being, at least – Prince Rainier composed his differences with Onassis and gave him his full support. Livanos was forced to withdraw from the contest and the rival he had petulantly tried to oust was left in a stronger position than ever.*

Thanks largely to Princess Grace, the pigeon-shooting was put a stop to at last. But an ingenious device was installed in its place; marksmen could show their skill and compete for large prizes by blazing away at flying and mobile quarries whose propeller equipment and trajectory and variation of speed convincingly simulated the flight of live birds. Innovations like this were aimed at an easy-going and less exalted and, above all, less obviously prosperous public. Prince Rainier felt even more should be done to encourage middle-income visitors and suggested that the company reverted to the practice of providing free drinks and entertainment, as François and Camille Blanc had done. 'No one now wants to walk into a gambling room as though it were a cathedral,' he said. 'In Las Vegas a fellow quits the table and goes to the bar, where he finds a few girls waiting to be asked to dance, and he doesn't pay for his drink – it's on the house.' Onassis did not share this opinion. Economically, he considered the company could not even afford its present outlay. The casino was seriously overmanned. One thousand two hundred Monégasques (out of an electorate of only two thousand) were employed by the company, where nine hundred would have been enough. But the prince was under constant pressure to keep these subjects on and it was impossible to reduce the staff to normal size. Despite the prince's plea for free drinks, the casino continued to charge clients even for

* This version of what happened conflicts, however, with Onassis's own statement that he had acquired an absolute majority of the shares several months before the movement on the bourse.

a bottle of mineral water, so it was not surprising that another idea – floodlighting the tennis courts for playing at night during the heat of the summer – was turned down too.

The prince also criticized Onassis for encouraging what he called shows and jazz bands instead of cultural activities – the budget for the opera, for instance, had not been increased for years – and yet putting this vulgar entertainment out of reach of all but the rich by the exorbitant prices charged in the company's nightclubs. In the heat of the debate Onassis said he thought gambling in Monte Carlo was immoral and the prince replied that Onassis was in no position to lecture anyone on morality.

Another source of discord was the proliferation of one-armed bandits. The prince would have liked them all in one room, and preferably underground, instead of scattered all over the casino and also in the Café de Paris, which had recently been turned into a drugstore in the American style; but the company argued that since the machines were so profitable – only two men were needed to look after fifty, with a third to open the boxes and collect the money – there should be as many as possible everywhere.

These disagreements were reflected in the management of the company, and when Onassis asked the prince to amend his power of veto or to waive it – it was unsound, he argued, to seek investment in a concern which was at the mercy of an individual whim – the prince suggested that Onassis should sell out and take his interests elsewhere.

In November 1962 Onassis did in fact offer the prince his entire holding. Ostensibly this was to bolster the prince's position in the face of growing pressure from France to impose taxes on the commercial and industrial companies operating in Monaco. 'I gave Prince Rainier a ninety-day option,' he subsequently explained. 'I did it because of his difficulties with the French government. I wanted to help him.' But since he was asking ten thousand francs for each of his shares – almost double the market value – this offer was understandably turned down and the option expired. In any case, the only measure the French had taken was to put up customs barriers on the roads and check the traffic entering and leaving the principality, and even this was lifted six months later. The prince conceded that Monaco-based companies with a turnover of more than twenty-five per cent in France should be subjected to a profits tax of twenty-five per cent. French subjects of less than five years' residence became liable to income tax.

Dozens of firms had meanwhile followed Onassis' example and taken up their headquarters in Monte Carlo. The result was a giant building boom. As land was so scarce, skyscrapers and many-storied concrete blocks sprouted from every available site and were soon shooting aloft until they dwarfed the casino and transformed the principality into a miniature Manhattan. The scrapping of the old overland railway line provided further building space. All this served to widen the rift between the company and the government, and in February 1965, in a broadcast on the Monte Carlo radio station, the prince openly attacked the company for making the principality a hunting-ground for building speculation. Onassis, he said, was aiming to split the SBM into three different companies – one for the gambling, a second for auxiliary exploitation, and a third for real estate – with a view to farming out the gambling, the hotels and the entertainment in concessions to other businessmen, while he maintained control of the holding company and made large profits on real estate deals with the casino's land. This scheme, the prince claimed, would ruin the company and consequently the whole economy of the principality. He himself, on the contrary, wished to make the economy more democratic by building medium-class hotels for mass tourism. Onassis argued that this would drive away for ever the two or three hundred very rich patrons who were the mainstay of the casino.

By the summer of 1965 hints were being dropped about the possibility of nationalizing the company. These were countered by fresh rumours that Onassis was preparing to sell out. The situation was aptly summed up by the *Sunday Telegraph*:

By holding 520,000 of the million shares in the SBM, Mr Onassis would seem to be in an impregnable position compared with the prince. But if the prince is a 'minnow' in the share pool he holds the trump card of being Head of State and able to wield greater power by legal means ... Should Mr Onassis decide to sell his interests he would reap a rich reward. The current stock exchange quotation stands at about 69 francs* (£5) a share. As he paid between 7s. and 15s. a share for his original purchase, his profit would run into millions of pounds.

The prince clarified his position in a later interview:

> The State at the moment has a very small amount of shares in the SBM – about twenty thousand. I inherited twenty-two thousand personally from my family. So, as a sharehloder, I have really little importance and am in no position to throw my weight about. But as Prince of Monaco I can – as long as I don't damage the company's interests ... The only thing now which is very good is that the National Council is angry with the SBM and ready, if necessary, to vote a law of complete national-ization.

1966 was the centenary of the naming of Monte Carlo. On 27 May the croupiers held a two-hour strike in a dispute over how to share the tips when the blackjack tables were installed. No details were announced as to the eventual agreement 'because,' it was darkly stated, 'of the ultra-secrecy of the croupier's profession'. The year was marked by an event of greater importance. A bill was passed on 23 June, which gave each shareholder the chance to sell his holding to the state at a fixed price of eighty francs a share. It also provided an increase in the company's capital from five million to eight million francs by the issue of a block of six hundred thousand shares to be subscribed by the Monaco government. An extraordinary meeting of the shareholders also endorsed a proposal to issue one new share for every five held. Thus the capital was raised to nine million francs, distributed in 1,800,000 shares. The bill did not give the state a majority holding – the government still controlled only thirty per cent of the total shares – but it did deprive Onassis of *his* majority. He therefore

---

* The new franc, worth 100 old francs, had been introduced on 1 January 1963.

took his case before the Monaco supreme court. He appealed against the new law and accused the government of using unconstitutional means. At the same time he announced that he would resign from the administration of the company.

The hearing began on 27 February 1967, and Onassis' lawyer argued that the new statute was an infringement of the right of private property. He also contended that the notion of the SBM's providing a 'public service' as laid down in the original statutes no longer held good. For all his eloquence, the court rejected the appeal, and the long conflict came to an end on 17 March when the Monaco treasury wrote a cheque to Onassis for the sum of 39,912,000 francs.

A profit of thirty-five million francs would have seemed handsome to most financiers, but not to Onassis. Shortly after taking over the SBM he had boasted that for five million francs he had got control of a property worth one hundred million in real estate alone. So it was disappointing and humiliating to be fobbed off with a third of it. His final comment was: 'We were gypped.'

When Onassis withdrew, Monte Carlo embarked on a new and more precarious phase. The casino had long ceased to be the mainstay of the economy, and though the prince and the Monaco government were now in full control of the company neither had the money for investment on the Onassis scale. In the hope of attracting American finance, Marcel Palmero, a senior partner in the New York banking firm of Lehmann Brothers, and consul-general of Monaco in New York, was appointed president of the SBM.

In spite of an elaborate scheme to reclaim land and create new residential areas and artificial beaches, tourism had already begun to decline. There was a dearth of British visitors in particular; their travel allowance had lately been reduced to £50 by the Labour government's credit squeeze; even during the Monte Carlo Rally the casino, according to *The Times* (21 January 1967), had an air of emptiness and depression that was shattering compared with the bustling, free-spending atmosphere of a year ago'. By June 1968 things had deteriorated still further. Ninety-eight per cent of the workers in the cafés and restaurants and hotels went on a twenty-four-hour strike for better wages and conditions. Two years later another strike, in support of wage demands by the humbler stratum of the casino's staff, closed down the gaming rooms and spread once again to the principal hotels and restaurants. And in 1973 the croupiers again went on strike in protest at the closed-circuit television system which had been installed for extra security. It was a slur on their honour, they said. But, thanks to the prince's policy, the economy recovered and the hundred and sixty million francs receipts of 1974 rose to a hundred and ninety-five next year.

The increase had been helped along during the previous October by the one-week visit of three Saudi-Arabian princes. Special concessions were made and the gaming-rooms, which normally closed at 2 am, were kept open as long as they wanted and sometimes until nine o'clock in the morning. The maximum stake was quadrupled at their request: by pooling their bets, they stood to win more than a quarter of a million francs at one spin of the wheel. They did win heavily at first – ten million francs – but by the end of the week they had gambled it away and lost thirty million more.

In Monte Carlo nowadays gambling on such a spectacular scale is rare. 'Business tycoons and international stars have taken the place of Russian grand dukes,' says the casino, but the average customer is a much less glamorous figure. The 'kitchen' is still frequented every morning by faded old ladies and seedy old gentlemen who make a modest living by staking small sums in accordance with a simple system. In looks, these faithful votaries – *les licenciés ès roulette*, as the croupiers affectionately call them – have not changed much since Monte Carlo's heyday. But the elegant and fashionable figures of that golden age have vanished for ever; and even in the *salles privées*, in the evening and at the height of the season, slacks are allowed for women and men no longer have to wear ties. The appearance of these latter-day clients jars painfully with an old-fashioned décor which has been so conscientiously preserved that two ghosts from the *belle époque* would recognize their surroundings in a second.

But the outside of the building would be strange to them. From many angles it would now be entirely masked by the encroachments of the modern town and even from the sea it would no longer look the same. The twin-towered landmark of the theatre grows blurred among a background of skyscrapers, and the view may be blocked out soon by the mushroom urbanization of land reclaimed on its seaward side. François Blanc and Charles Garnier could never have foreseen this when they drew up their plans.

CASINO GAMES

Roulette

This is by far the most popular game at Monte Carlo, not only because the minimum stake – ten francs in the 'kitchen', twenty francs in the *salles privées* – is half that at trente-et-quarante, but also because it offers the player a variety of chances and combinations of chances. On the other hand it affords less favourable odds than trente-et-quarante.

THE WHEEL

The roulette machine consists of a shallow circular basin made of wood, the bottom of which is formed by a separate metal disc mounted on a pivot (see Figure A). The inward sloping side of the basin is fitted with fourteen equidistant diamond-shaped brass studs – seven vertical and seven horizontal in relation to the wheel – and round its upper edge there is a deep oval moulding. The wheel, always referred to by the croupiers as '*le cylindre*', is divided into thirty-seven identical compartments numbered from 0 to 36 in an apparently haphazard manner and coloured red and black alternately. Zero, which ranks as colourless, lies between 26 black and 32 red (see Figure B). These compartments, which are marked off by means of slightly raised metal ridges, are situated near the circumference, and from them a bevelled surface slopes gently upwards towards the central point on the disc which is fitted with a small cross-shaped brass handle.

The apparently haphazard numbering of the compartments is

FIGURE A

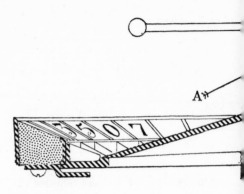

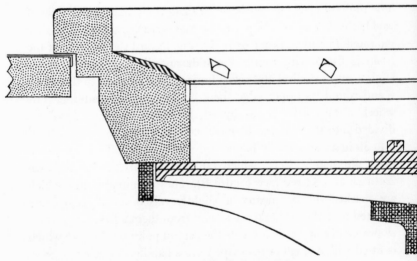

CROSS-SECTION OF A ROULETTE WHEEL

From a constructor's drawing

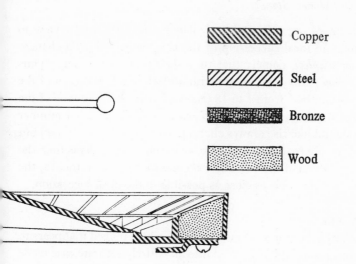

Copper

Steel

Bronze

Wood

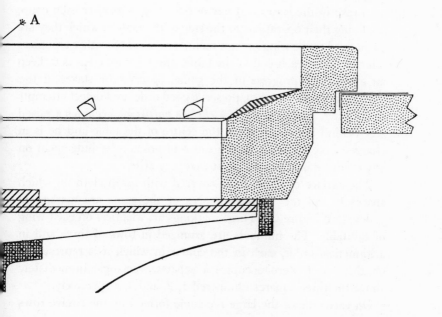

A

in fact based on a carefully calculated principle, with a view to obtaining an ideal succession of the three so-called even chances (*chances simples*), namely that they shall occur alternately. Thus a red (*rouge*) always alternates with a black (*noir*), and each of the eighteen numbers from 1 to 18 (*manque*) alternates with one of the eighteen numbers from 19 to 36 (*passe*). Ideally an even number (*pair*) should likewise always alternate with an uneven (*impair*) but this strict alternation cannot be achieved without affecting the ideal succession of the two other *chances simples*. Nevertheless, the *pair-impair* chance is as close as possible to the ideal succession.

THE TABLE

The wheel is not placed *on* the table, of which indeed it appears to be an integral part, but is fitted into an entirely separate case made of bronze or gunmetal which is firmly fixed to the floor independently of the large wooden surface surrounding it. This central section is narrower than the rest of the table, so that a curved 'waist' is formed between the two main wings, affording enough room for two croupiers to sit together on each side. It is these four who rake in the losses and pay out the winnings after each coup, confining their operations to the side of the table at which they are sitting and to the wing nearest them. There are two other croupiers who sit one at each end of the table, and their function is to keep an eye on the progress of the game, observe the stakes of the players, prevent mistakes, preserve good order and detect attempts at cheating. Finally there is a *chef de partie*; he occupies a raised seat behind the croupiers at the centre of the table and he is in charge of the progress of the game and pronounces judgement on any doubtful or disputed point that may arise.

The surface of the table is covered with green cloth on which spaces for all the various chances of the game are marked in yellow (see Figure C). These markings are identical on each wing of the table. The numbers are arranged in rows of three and in arithmetical order, each in the colour in which it is represented on the wheel. Zero occupies a separate rectangle immediately above the three squares numbered 1, 2, and 3, respectively.

On each side of the large rectangle formed by the twelve rows

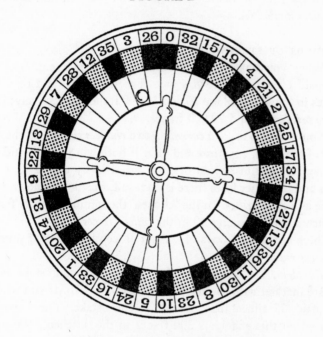

FIGURE B

PLAN OF A ROULETTE WHEEL

of numerals there are three large spaces for the three pairs of
chances simples; each of these spaces is inscribed with the name
of the chance it represents, except the pair reserved for *rouge* and
noir which, instead of being inscribed respectively with those
words, are marked with a red diamond-shaped figure and a
corresponding black one. Near the outer edge of each of these six
spaces, and running parallel to it, is a vertical line marking the
boundary for such stakes as are impounded, or put *en prison*, on
the occurrence of zero.

Immediately below the rows of numerals there are three small
unmarked rectangles for the reception of stakes laid on one or
another of the three vertical columns; and on either side of these
rectangles are three small spaces marked 12 P, 12 M and 12 D,
respectively, which are reserved for the stakes laid on the first

dozen (*première douzaine*), middle dozen (*milieu*), and last dozen (*dernière douzaine*).

METHODS OF STAKING

A. When you stake on any of the *chances simples*, e.g. *passe*, you are paid even money if you win. The minimum and maximum stakes in the 'kitchen' are 10 and 10,000 francs respectively; in the *salles privées*, 20 and 20,000 francs.

B. You may also stake *à cheval* on two *chances simples* on the same side of the table, e.g. *passe* and *pair*. If both win you are paid even money. If both lose, your stake is raked in by the bank. If one wins and the other loses there is no result, this being known in the game as a *coup neutre*. In the 'kitchen' the minimum stake for this chance is 20 francs and 40 in the *salles privées*.

There are several ways of staking on combinations of numbers (*chances multiples*):

C. *En plein*, i.e. on one number. You place your stake in the square marked with the relevant numeral, e.g. 16. If you win you are paid 35 times the amount of your stake. The maximum allowed on this chance is 300 francs in the 'kitchen', 600 in the *salles privées*.

D. *A cheval*, i.e. in two adjacent numbers. You place your stake on the partition line between the two numbers, e.g. 19–22. (The fancied resemblance of its position to a man's seat on horseback accounts for the term *à cheval*.) Win: 17 times the stake.

E. *Transversale*, i.e. on one of the horizontal rows of three numbers, e.g. 25–26–27. You place your stake on the line dividing the row from the adjacent space reserved for the *chance simple*. Win: 11 times the stake.

F. *Carré*, i.e. on a square composed of four adjacent numbers, e.g. 31–32–34–35. You place your stake on the intersection of the two arms of the cross formed by the lines dividing the four numbers. Win: 8 times the stake.

G. *Quatre premiers*, i.e. on the first four numbers, 0–1–2–3. You place your stake on either end of the line dividing the space reserved for zero from the first horizontal row. Win: 8 times the stake.

FIGURE C

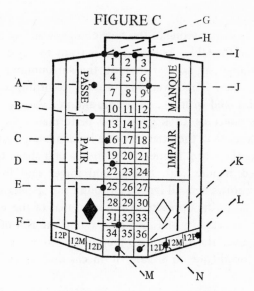

PLAN OF A ROULETTE TABLE

H. and I. Zero can also be played in combination with any one or two of its neighbours, e.g. 0–1 or 0–2–3. If with one of them, i.e. *à cheval*, payment for a win is 17 times the stake; if with two the win is 11 times the stake.

J. *Sixain*, i.e. on two adjacent horizontal rows of numbers, e.g. 4–5–6–7–8–9. You place your stake on either end of the line dividing the two rows. Win: 5 times the stake.

K. *Colonne*, i.e. on one of the three vertical columns of twelve numbers. You place your stake in the small square immediately below the column. Win: double the amount of the stake.

L. *Douzaine*, i.e. on one of the three dozens, e.g. the first. You place your stake in the small space marked 12 P. Win: double the amount of the stake.

M. and N. You may also stake *à cheval* on two adjacent columns or two adjacent dozens. You are paid when one of the numbers included in either of the two columns or either of the two dozens comes out. Win: half the amount of the stake.

PROCEDURE

The wheel is spun by one of the four croupiers sitting together at the middle of the table. As soon as he is ready he says: *'Messieurs, faites vos jeux'*,* by way of inviting the surrounding players to place their stakes. 'This invariable formula,' according to an expert, 'is usually intoned with a nasal twang, and in a voice so colourless and monotonous as to suggest the performance of a talking machine rather than the utterance of a human being.' At the same time he sets the wheel in motion by means of a sharp turn of the cross-shaped handle with thumb and finger and immediately afterwards throws a small ivory ball round the sloping side of the wooden basin in the opposite direction to that of the wheel. The marble is prevented by the moulding round the rim of the basin from flying over the side and as long as its momentum is maintained, in obedience to a law of mechanics, it continues its course.

As long as it is sustained by the action of this centrifugal force and continues to revolve round the side of the basin, stakes may be placed or changed. But as its momentum declines and its velocity decreases, it leaves the rim and runs down the incline until, just before reaching the spinning wheel, it strikes the diamond-shaped metal studs situated round the basin and, under the force of this collision, its movement becomes irregular and arbitrary. At this point the croupier says: *'Les jeux sont faits, rien ne va plus,'* and no further stake is allowed to be placed.

When the ball at last reaches the spinning wheel, it encounters further obstructions in the shape of the raised metal edges marking

* He never says, *'Mesdames et messieurs'*, even when, as is nowadays usually the case, ladies are present at the table. This tradition dates from the time when it was considered unseemly for women to gamble. Croupiers also frequently use the term *'louis'* when announcing bets, though this coin has been out of currency for half a century. There are other terms in frequent use which may bewilder the novice. For instance, a player may hand a croupier three 10-franc chips (or, for that matter, a 50-franc note, change for which will be promptly provided) and say, *'Finales sept par dix.'* The croupier will then place the chips on 7, 17 and 27 – these numbers all ending in seven. More rarely a request may be made for, say, *'Tiers du cylindre sud-est par cent'*, in which case the croupier will place six 100-franc chips *à cheval* on 6–8, 10–11, 13–16, 21–14, 27–30 and 33–36 – these numbers occurring in the south-eastern section of the wheel.

off the numbered compartments, whereupon its path becomes even more uncertain and erratic; but it still has sufficient impetus to clear these obstacles and run up the bevelled surface at the centre of the wheel before rolling back again into one of the compartments where it finally comes to rest.

The result is immediately proclaimed by the officiating croupier, and invariably in the following order: first the number itself, then the winning side of each of the three *chances simples*. If the winning number is 19, for example, he announces: '*Dix-neuf, rouge, impair et passe.*' Should it be 22, he would say: '*Vingt-deux, noir, pair et passe.*' He and his colleagues then rake in the losing stakes and start paying out the winners.

THE REFAIT

If the ball falls into the compartment numbered 0, the croupier announces '*Zéro,*' and he and his colleagues rake in all the stakes placed on numbers and groups of numbers except those on 0 itself and on the combinations including 0, i.e. the *quatre premiers* and 0-1-2, 0-2-3, 0-2 and 0-3. The stakes on dozens and columns are also raked in, and those on the *chances simples* are put *en prison*, namely moved to the edge of the table on the outer side of the line running parallel to it. (Alternatively you have the option of forfeiting half your stake.) If you win the next coup you are out of prison, your stake is moved back into the centre of the space of the *chance simple* on which you placed it, and you have the option of taking it up or allowing it to remain. This advantage to the bank is called the *refait*.

The percentage of the gross amount staked, which the bank secures for itself by means of the *refait*, may be calculated by applying the Law of Probabilities. The probability that 0 will come out in any coup is $\frac{1}{37}$ since there are 37 numbers, including zero. The action of the *refait* is therefore to divert the 37th part of the stakes on the *chances multiples* and the 74th part of those on the *chances simples* to the bank, i.e. from every 100 francs staked upon the *chances multiples* $\frac{100}{37}$ or 2.70 francs, from every hundred francs

staked on the *chances simples* $\frac{100}{74}$ or 1.35 francs. So the advantage
to the bank is 2.7 per cent on all amounts staked on the *chances
multiples*, and 1.35 per cent on all stakes on the *chances simples*. It is
therefore, mathematically, in your interest to stake on *chances
simples* rather than on *chances multiples*.

Trente-et-Quarante

This is essentially the richer man's game, the minimum and maximum stakes being double those at roulette, i.e. 20 and 20,000
francs respectively in the 'kitchen', and 50 and 50,000 francs in the
salles privées. It is also the game preferred by the more serious
gambler, since the advantage to the bank at trente-et-quarante is
less than that at roulette. Finally it is the simpler game of the two
since it offers in all only four chances, namely two pairs of equal
alternatives or *chances simples – pair-impair* and *couleur-inverse*.

THE TABLE

This is similar to the roulette table, with a 'waist' or curved break
in the middle of each side, where the *chef de partie* and four
croupiers sit. (In view of the simplicity of the game, the two
croupiers on duty one at each end of the roulette table are dis-
pensed with at trente-et-quarante.) The croupier charged with the
shuffling and dealing of the cards is called the *tailleur*, and in front
of him is a slotted metal container let into the table into which he
throws the cards that have been used.

The surface of the table is covered with green cloth divided into
several spaces with lines drawn in yellow (see Figure D). The two
largest spaces, on the outer edges, and marked with a red diamond-
shaped figure and a black one respectively, are reserved for the
stakes placed on *rouge* and on *noir*, since this pair of chances is far
more popular with players than *couleur* and *inverse*, although the
probabilities are in fact identical for both pairs. Between these

spaces are two lines starting from the centre of the table and running parallel to each other at first but bending inwards lower down so that they intersect and form an angle. These enclose two irregular spaces for the stakes placed on *couleur* and on *inverse* – the pentagon being reserved for the former, and the triangle for the latter.

FIGURE D

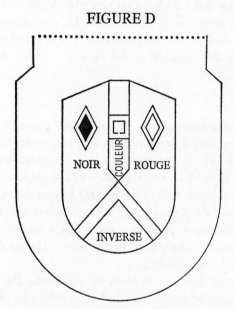

PLAN OF A TRENTE-ET-QUARANTE TABLE

RULES OF THE GAME

Trente-et-quarante is played with six packs of ordinary playing-cards. These are dealt in two horizontal rows, each of which, when complete, must represent in points a number between 31 and 40, and to which no further addition is made when the total points of the cards composing it have reached any number above 30. Each of the court cards counts as ten, each of the others at its face value, including the ace which counts as one. The upper row of cards decides for the chance *noir*, the lower for the chance *rouge*. The winning row is the one with the smaller number of points. If, for example, the upper row contains 37 points and the lower 32, *rouge* wins.

The chances *couleur* and *inverse* are determined by the first card dealt in each coup, i.e. by the first card in the upper row. If this is of the same colour as the winning row, *couleur* wins; if it is of the opposite colour, *inverse* wins.

You may also stake *à cheval* on any two chances which do not belong to the same pair of alternatives, i.e. on *noir-couleur, noir-inverse, rouge-couleur* and *rouge-inverse*. The amount so staked is placed on the line separating the spaces reserved for the two chances selected.

PROCEDURE

New cards are used for each game. Before play opens, the six sealed packs are shown to the players who may verify that the seals are intact. The *tailleur* then opens the packs and shuffles them, first one at a time, then all six together. One of the players is invited to cut the cards, a blank card being handed to him for this purpose. The cards are then placed in the 'shoe' (*sabot*) and the *tailleur* announces: '*Messieurs, faites vos jeux.*' After allowing sufficient time for the stakes to be placed he then says: '*Le jeu est fait, rien ne va plus,*' and starts dealing.

As soon as the first row is dealt, he announces the number of points it contains, or rather the number by which its total exceeds 30. For example, if the cards composing it represent 35 points, he proclaims: '*Cinq.*' It is only when they represent forty points that he announces the whole number, '*Quarante.*' When the second row has been dealt he announces the points it contains in the same way and, in addition, the result of the coup, i.e. which chance in each of the pairs of alternatives has won and which lost; but, in accordance with tradition, he never mentions *noir* or *inverse* in this announcement. For example, if black wins and colour loses, he says: '*Rouge perd, et couleur,*' the other three possible results being announced respectively as: '*Rouge gagne, et couleur,*' '*Rouge gagne et couleur perd,*' and '*Rouge perd et couleur gagne.*'

After each deal he slips the cards into the slot of the metal container. When there are not enough left to complete the two rows, he announces: '*Les cartes passent.*' They are then taken from the container, reshuffled, and another game begins.

THE REFAIT

If the number of points represented by each of the two rows of cards is the same (e.g. 35, in which case the *tailleur* announces: '*Cinq après*'), the coup does not count and is said to be *nul* – unless this number is 31. The occurrence of 31 in each of the two rows constitutes the refait.* In this case the *tailleur* announces: '*Un après,*' and all the stakes are impounded or put *en prison*, those laid on *rouge* or on *noir* being moved to the red and the black diamond-shaped spaces respectively, those on *couleur* to the small quadrangle above the pentagon, and those on *inverse* to the chevron-shaped space above the triangle. Alternatively, as at roulette, you have the option of forfeiting half your stake.

The probability of a *refait* occurring at trente-et-quarante may be calculated precisely, but this calculation is more complicated than in the case of roulette.

A row may be brought up to 31 by the addition to it of any one of the thirteen different cards contained in a pack: by an ace, for example, if the number of points already reached is 30; by a two if it is 29; by a three if it is 28; and so on. But a row cannot possibly be completed to 32 by an ace; nor to 33 by an ace or a two; nor to 34 by an ace, a two or a three; and so on. From this it can be seen that rows of 31 will occur most frequently (for which reason, no doubt, the number in question was chosen for the *refait*); and rows of 40, which can be completed only by a ten or a court card, will occur most seldom of all.

The following table may therefore be constructed, giving the mathematical probability as to the comparative frequency with which each of the numbers between 31 and 40 will occur:

---

* The demi-refait was a novelty introduced by François Blanc at Homburg to attract 'serious players'. Stakes were impounded only when both rows of cards came to 31 *and* the last card in each row was black. But this concession is not made in any casino today.

Rows of 31 will occur on average 13 times

,,	,, 32	,,	,,	,,	,,	12	,,
,,	,, 33	,,	,,	,,	,,	11	,,
,,	,, 34	,,	,,	,,	,,	10	,,
,,	,, 35	,,	,,	,,	,,	9	,,
,,	,, 36	,,	,,	,,	,,	8	,,
,,	,, 37	,,	,,	,,	,,	7	,,
,,	,, 38	,,	,,	,,	,,	6	,,
,,	,, 39	,,	,,	,,	,,	5	,,
,,	,, 40	,,	,,	,,	,,	4	,,

Total: 85

From this it may be seen that out of 85 rows of cards dealt, 13 of them will probably be rows of 31. In other words, the probability of a row coming out with 31 points is $\frac{13}{85}$. Now since the probability of a single row containing 31 points is $\frac{13}{85}$, the probability that both rows will contain this number of points is $\frac{13}{85} \times \frac{13}{85} = \frac{169}{7225}$, or, in other words, in 7,225 coups the *refait* will probably occur 169 times. Similarly since the probability of a single row containing 32 points is $\frac{12}{85}$, the probability that both rows will contain this number of points, i.e. *deux après*, is $\frac{12}{85} \times \frac{12}{85} = \frac{144}{7225}$. And this formula may be applied to determine the probable frequency of all the other *coups nuls*. Furthermore the probable frequency of every possible combination besides *coups nuls* may also be determined by the same formula, e.g. since the probable frequency of a row of 31 is $\frac{13}{85}$, and that of a row of 40 is $\frac{4}{85}$, the probable frequency of this combination is $\frac{13}{85} \times \frac{4}{85} = \frac{52}{7225}$.

The following table may therefore be constructed, giving the probable frequency of each of these possible combinations:

After	31	32	33	34	35	36	37	38	39	40
31 ,,	169	156	143	130	117	104	91	78	65	52
32 ,,	156	144	132	120	108	96	84	72	60	48
33 ,,	143	132	121	110	99	88	77	66	55	44
34 ,,	130	120	110	100	90	80	70	60	50	40
35 ,,	117	108	99	90	81	72	63	54	45	36
36 ,,	104	96	88	80	72	64	56	48	40	32
37 ,,	91	84	77	70	63	56	49	42	35	28
38 ,,	78	72	66	60	54	48	42	36	30	24
39 ,,	65	60	55	50	45	40	35	30	25	02
40 ,,	52	48	44	40	36	32	28	24	20	16
7,225	1105	1020	935	850	765	680	595	510	425	340

From this table it can be seen that in 7,225 coups the *refait* will probably occur 169 times, while the probable frequency of *coups nuls* is as follows:

Deux après:	144
Trois après:	121
Quatre après:	100
Cinq après:	81
Six après:	64
Sept après:	49
Huit après:	36
Neuf après:	25
Quarante après:	16
	——
Total:	636

Now since, in 7,225 coups, the average number of *refaits* is 169 and the average number of *coups nuls* is 636, the average number of valid coups must be 6,589. The proportion of *refaits* to valid coups is therefore 169 to 6,589. In other words, 2.56 per cent of the valid coups will result in the *refait*. Now, since the bank takes one half of the stakes when the *refait* occurs, the advantage it thereby derives is 1.28 per cent of the amounts staked on all four chances.

This advantage is 1.42 per cent less than the bank derives from the *chances multiples*, and only 0.07 per cent less than it derives from the *chances simples*, at roulette. Yet considering the apparently small advantage to the bank is what has kept Monte Carlo in business for more than a century, a decrease in it of even 0.07 per cent represents a comparatively significant advantage to the player. It is therefore in your interest, mathematically, to play trente-et-quarante rather than roulette.

INSURING AGAINST THE REFAIT

At trente-et-quarante you are allowed to insure against the risk of a *refait* by paying a premium of 1 per cent of your stake – the minimum premium being, however, 5 francs. The procedure is to hand the croupier your insurance fee and say: '*Assurez la pièce* (or) *la masse*', i.e.: 'Insure the chip (or) the pile of chips', whichever your stake may be; whereupon the croupier replies: '*La pièce* (or) *la masse est assurée*', and throws a small white counter on to your stake.

The argument in favour of this insurance is that since the *refait* represents an advantage to the bank of 1.28 per cent, a fee of only 1 per cent is cheap and advantageous to the player. According to some authorities, however, this argument is erroneous. Victor Silberer, for example, contends that since the *refait* does not entail the loss of your whole stake, but only half of it, the premium of 1 per cent does not insure the whole amount staked but only half of it. In effect, therefore, you are paying a premium of 2 per cent – which is higher than the normal advantage to the bank of 1.28 per cent.

Whichever way you look at it, since the minimum premium is 5 francs, it is not in your interest to insure a stake of less than 500.

Baccara

Just as the name of this game is spelt in two different ways, *baccara* and *baccarat*, so there are two different versions of it – *baccara banque* (or *à deux tableaux*) and *baccara chemin-de-fer*.

Furthermore the former version, which the French sometimes call *tout va*, is generally referred to by the English as plain *baccara*; while the latter, which the French commonly call plain *baccara*, is usually known to the English as plain *chemin-de-fer* or 'chemmy'. Both, however, are essentially the same game.

BACCARA BANQUE

Unlike roulette or trente-et-quarante, where each individual plays against the bank, at baccara you stake against one individual banker. The latter is simply the player who says he will put up the most money for the others to play against. In principle, therefore, the stakes are limited to what that particular player can afford. In practice, however, they tend to be extremely high since the banker usually represents a syndicate whose funds and expertise are sufficient to daunt all but the wealthiest and most intrepid gambler. Such were the resources and confidence of the famous Greek Syndicate, for instance, that in 1922, its representative at Deauville was able to announce '*Tout va*' – hence one of the alternative names of the game – and from then on the sky was the limit.

No casino in the world could afford to hold the bank at baccara on these terms. The Greek Syndicate was able to do so only by playing at several casinos, so that what they lost at one they might win back at another. Since the end of the Second World War the Monte Carlo casino has in fact been holding the bank, or running its own syndicate, at baccara. But the maximum at the table is limited to 150,000 francs, and the stakes are of 500 francs or any multiple thereof up to 5,000. Strictly speaking, therefore, baccara at Monte Carlo cannot be described as *tout va*, but it is still *par excellence* the very rich man's game. For this reason it is played at only one table and during only two sessions a day: before and after dinner.

PROCEDURE

Baccara is played at an oval table covered in a green baize cloth which is divided into two halves, or *tableaux*, by a line across the centre, at one end of which sits the banker and at the other the croupier in charge of the game. Six new packs of cards are used at each of the two sessions. Before the game starts they are spread face down on the table and shuffled by the croupier, who then hands the player on his right a blank card with which to cut them. Finally they are placed in the 'shoe' or *sabot*, from which the banker deals them one by one.

Before the deal begins, any player may bet, by placing his stake on one side of the table or the other, that the hand dealt to the one *tableaux* or the other will beat the dealer's; or, alternatively, *à cheval* (in which case he places his stake on the line across the centre of the table) that the hands dealt to both *tableau* will win. The winning hand is the one that hold cards adding up to nine or a number most closely approaching nine. Tens and court cards count as nothing; all others are reckoned at their face value.

The banker starts by dealing one card face down to the player on his right, then another to the player on his left, and finally a third to himself. Then he deals another three cards in the same order.

None of the other players receive cards. They win or lose according to the hand of the player representing their particular *tableau*. If, for example, the player on the right of the banker wins, then all the players sitting on that side of the table win. Each of the representative players has the right to continue playing for his *tableau* until that *tableau* loses a coup, when the next player in precedence on that side takes over from him. But the latter (and any player) may forgo his right to play and let the next in precedence take over instead.

After the deal each of the players examines the cards he has received. The banker likewise examines the hand he has dealt himself. Any of them having a 'natural', e.g. a pair of fours or any other combination making eight, or a six and a three or any other combination making nine, must declare it and disclose his cards. If the other two cannot match his score, he wins. Ties neither win nor lose but go over to the next deal.

If any one of them does not have a natural, i.e. eight or nine, he does not disclose his hand and may draw a third card, which is dealt face up, depending on the two he already holds. If the first player does not accept another card, the banker offers it to the second player, who may likewise refuse or accept it, and he then decides whether or not to draw himself. The one whose score is nearest to nine wins the coup. The croupier then slips the used cards into the slotted metal container let into the table, and the banker deals again. This procedure is repeated until there are fewer than nine cards left in the 'shoe'.

GAMESMANSHIP
If either player's cards add up to four or less (and for the purpose of the game tens are deducted when the points reach double figures, so that a seven and a six, making thirteen, count as three) he must logically take another card, since any from an ace to a five will improve his score. If his hand adds up to six or seven, he must similarly not accept another card, since only an ace, a two or a three can help him. If it adds up to five, he has the option of standing or drawing. The banker therefore has the advantage of being able in advance to make a rough calculation of each of his opponent's hands and will decide whether to draw or stand accordingly.

If, for example, both players stand, he knows they both have a score of five and over. He must then logically also stand if his own hand is six or seven, since only an ace or a two can improve it in relation to either of theirs. But he must logically draw if his own hand is five or under, since otherwise his score is less than, or at best only equals, either of theirs.

If, however, either of them draws a third card, his decision will depend on the value of that card in relation to his own hand. By applying the same logical process as for his simpler decision, the table on page 164 may be constructed.

As can be seen, therefore, the option of standing or drawing is a decisive factor in the game for each of the two players as well as for the banker. Mathematically a player standing on five has a better chance of winning than if he draws to that score; for if he draws there are only four cards (an ace, a two, a three or a four) that can improve it, while there are five (a five, a six, a seven, an eight or a nine) that will impair it. In practice it has been calculated that by standing he has a 51.23 per cent chance of winning;

while if he draws, his chance of winning is only 50.06 per cent. For this reason most players stand.

It has also been calculated that for a banker holding three and giving his opponent a nine, his chance of winning is about 60 per cent if he stands and only about 59 per cent if he draws. But these

If the banker gives	he must logically stand on	and draw to
0 or 1	4, 5, 6, and 7	0, 1, 2, and 3
2 or 3	5, 6, and 7	0, 1, 2, 3, and 4
4	5, 6, and 7	0, 1, 2, 3, 4, and 5*
5	6 and 7	0, 1, 2, 3, 4, and 5
6 or 7	7	0, 1, 2, 3, 4, 5, and 6
8	4, 5, 6, and 7	0, 1, 2, and 3
9	3, 4, 5, 6, and 7	0, 1, 2, and 3*

approximate chances are calculated on the assumption that his opponent will stand on five. Against a player who draws to five, he has a slight advantage if he himself draws, his chance of winning then being about 58.5 per cent. Similarly if he holds five and gives his opponent a three, he improves his chance of winning (but only by about 0.02 per cent) by standing – again assuming that his opponent will stand on five. Against a player who draws to five, his chance of winning is improved by about 0.06 per cent if he himself draws.

These calculations, however, are also conditioned by other considerations – for example, by the value of the cards already dealt, which, if he remembers every deal, might affect a player's decision – and the banker will then make *his* decision accordingly. Furthermore, since he has to play his one hand against those of two different opponents, he may also have to make a choice between two conflicting decisions. In this case, too, his calculations will be determined by other considerations – for example, if the stakes on one *tableau* are much larger than on the other, he may decide to sacrifice his chance of winning the smaller stakes in the hope of increasing his chance of winning the larger.

* He has the option of standing or drawing when his own hand comes to 3, and his opponent draws a 9; or when it comes to 5 and his opponent draws a 4.

CHEMIN-DE-FER

The same rules apply to this game as to baccara, with the difference that in chemin-de-fer only two hands are dealt, one to the banker's opponent and one to himself; and every player in turn acts as banker, starting with the one sitting on the croupier's left.

The banker places before him the sum he wishes to stake and the players do likewise, making up the amount of his stake between them. If he wins the coup he retains the bank and continues to deal until he loses. When he loses, the 'shoe' is passed to the player on his left who in his turn becomes banker, and so on, the 'shoe' travelling round the table like a railway train – hence the name of the game.

Any player may also 'go bank', signifying his wish to do so before the deal by saying '*Banco*'. In this case he alone plays against the entire stake of the banker, who may decide to accept the challenge or pass the bank, in which case it is offered to the highest bidder. If the player who 'goes bank' is beaten by the banker, he may tackle him again by saying '*Suivi*'. If, on the other hand, he wishes to desist, another player may say '*Banco*', or '*Banco avec la table*', meaning that others may again make up the amount of the stake between them but that he will in any case undertake to cover it by himself.

At chemin-de-fer (but not at baccara banque) the casino takes five per cent of every winning bank after the first one, this levy being inserted in the *cagnotte* after each deal.

Craps

There are over sixty different versions of this game. The one played at Monte Carlo is the Idaho variety.

PROCEDURE

Two ordinary dice are used and are thrown by each player in turn. If the total of the spots on his first throw is 7 or 11, he wins and is paid even money. If this total is 2, 3 or 12, he loses but continues to throw the dice. If the total is any of the remaining six possible points, i.e. 4, 5, 6, 8, 9 or 10, he neither wins nor loses but continues to throw the dice until he duplicates his first throw, known as the 'point', on which he likewise wins even money, or until he throws 7, whereupon he loses and has to pass the dice to the player on his left.

Everyone else round the table can bet on the result and there are various methods of staking:

Win pays even money. You back the thrower of the dice and win or lose accordingly.

Lose pays even money. You bet *against* the thrower. Therefore on the first throw 2 and 12 are winners, 7 and 11 are losers, and 3 is a 'stand-off' or *coup neutre*. If 'point' turns up after the first throw you lose, but if 7 turns up you win.

Field pays even money. Any of the seven 'field' numbers are winners, the four others are losers.

Come pays even money. This can be played only after the first throw. Winners and losers are the same as for *Win*.

Don't Come pays even money. This, too, can be played only after the first throw. Winners and losers are the same as for *Lose*.

Big Six pays even money. Any combination totalling 6 is a winner. You lose on 7.

Big Eight pays even money. Any combination totalling 8 is a winner. You lose on 7.

Hardways pays seven to one. The exact combination of numbers you select, such as 5 and 3, is the winner. Any other combination and 7 are losers.

Craps pays seven to one. 2, 3 and 12 are winners, all other combinations are losers.

Seven pays seven to one. Any combination totalling 7 is a winner, all others are losers.

Eleven pays fifteen to one. Any combination totalling 11 is a winner, all others are losers.

PROBABILITIES

Since a dice has six faces, any number from 1 to 6 can be thrown. The number of combinations that can be thrown with two dice is therefore thirty-six, and any combination from 2 to 12 can be obtained. To obtain a total of 2 spots, for example, only one combination is possible: you must throw 1 with one dice and 1 with the other. To obtain 3, however, there are two possible combinations: 1 with one dice and 2 with the other, or 2 with one dice and 1 with the other. On the same principle, to obtain 4 there are three possible combinations, and so on. The following table shows all the possible combinations for every total:

Total:	2	3	4	5	6	7	8	9	10	11	12
Combinations	1 1	1 2	1 3	1 4	1 5	1 6	2 6	3 6	4 6	5 6	6 6
		2 1	3 1	4 1	5 1	6 1	6 2	6 3	6 4	6 5	
			2 2	2 3	2 4	2 5	3 5	4 5	5 5		
				3 2	4 2	5 2	5 3	5 4			
					3 3	3 4	4 4				
						4 3					

As can be seen, there is only one combination (out of thirty-six) to obtain a total of 2 or 12. But there are two possible combinations to obtain 3 or 11; three possible combinations to obtain 4 or 10; four to obtain 5 or 9, five to obtain 6 or 8, and six possible combinations to obtain a total of 7. Therefore the probability of throwing each of these totals is as follows:

Total of Throw	Probability
2 or 12	1/36
3 or 11	2/36 (or 1/18)
4 or 10	3/36 (or 1/12)
5 or 9	4/36 (or 1/9)
6 or 8	5/36
7	6/36 (or 1/6)

Accordingly, the probability of a player winning on his first throw, i.e. throwing 7 or 11, is 6/36 plus 2/36 = 8/36 (or 2/9). The probability of his losing, i.e. throwing 2, 3 or 12 is 1/36 plus 2/36 plus 1/36 = 4/36 (or 1/9). The chance that he will win or lose on the first throw is therefore 2/9 plus 1/9 = 3/9 (or 1/3); and the probability of his first throw being indecisive is 2/3.

Supposing his first throw is 8, for example. 8 then becomes his 'point', which he was to throw before throwing 7 in order to win.

Now, as we have seen, the chance of throwing 7 is 6/36; and the chance of throwing 8 is 5/36. That is to say, there are five chances of throwing 8, and six chances of throwing 7. Therefore the probability of throwing 8 before throwing 7 is 5/11, and the probability that 7 will appear first is 6/11. By this calculation the probability of throwing each of the possible points before throwing 7 is as follows:

Point	Probability
4 or 10	3/9 (or 1/3)
5 or 9	4/10 (or 2/5)
6 or 8	5/11

The probability, before the first throw is made, of a player winning on each of the possible 'points' is therefore as follows:

Point	Probability	
4 or 10	$3/36 \times 1/3$	1/36
5 or 9	$4/36 \times 2/5$	2/45
6 or 8	$5/36 \times 5/11$	25/396

The *total* probability of winning can therefore be calculated by adding the sum of the three probabilities listed above, each multiplied by 2, to the probability of winning on the first throw, i.e. 2/9. The result is 244/495, or 0.49293.

Supposing a player stakes 100 francs and is paid even money. If he wins, he rakes in 200 francs. Now the probability of his winning is 0.49293. Therefore his expectation is 200×0.49293, or 98.586 francs, so that he is paying 100 francs for 98.586 francs' worth of risk. He therefore loses in the long run 1.414 per cent of what he stakes – and this percentage is the bank's advantage at craps, compared to 1.28 per cent at trente-et-quarante and 1.35 per cent on the *chances simples* at roulette.

SYSTEMS, CHANCE
AND LUCK

By the time Monte Carlo was founded, the bogey of the infallible system had been finally laid to rest. Indeed, so certain was François Blanc of the impossibility of defeating the bank at roulette that he offered a million francs to anyone who could demonstrate a foolproof way of doing so. But of the many so-called infallible systems that have since been produced, all are infallible only in the regularity with which they have proved failures. Nevertheless there have always been system players. Dostoevsky observed them at Homburg, 'with ruled papers in their hands, whereon they set down the coups, calculated the chances, reckoned, staked – and lost exactly as we more simple mortals who played without any reckoning at all'.

Despite Dostoevsky's observations – and even he admitted that 'in the flow of fortuitous chances there is, if not a system, at all events a sort of order' – many system players have managed to eke out a modest living from roulette. By the turn of the century they were a familiar feature of the Monte Carlo 'kitchen'. 'Most of them are old ladies with parchment faces. They turn up regularly at the opening of the tables with little books and reticules and private rakes with which to place their rare stakes. They get absolutely no fun out of the game; but, after all, they earn more money than stone-breakers, and they earn it in greater comfort.' These were the forerunners of the *licenciés ès roulette* of today.

Even before the turn of the century roulette and trente-et-quarante had been scientifically studied by reputable mathematicians. But their findings were generally too abstruse for the layman to comprehend, and gullible and greedy gamblers continued to be lured by popular publications ranging from the facetious – 'This little book will be found no respector of persons; it will endeavour to cater for Mr and Mrs Limity Dincome as well as the Marquis of Splashington and the newest thing in Possible Plungers' – to the downright dishonest which promised a guaranteed profit of five hundred francs a day in return for an immediate payment to the anonymous author of fifteen thousand francs. Pamphlets with such titles as *The Art of Winning*, *The Only True Way*, *The Secret of Gaining Wealth*, were on sale at every bookstall. But these were of no more profit to the purchaser than the book which the eponymous hero of Voltaire's *Micromégas* gave to mankind in order to disclose the enigma of the universe but which, on being carried in ceremony to the Academy of Science and solemnly opened, was found to be full of blank paper.

Meanwhile gamblers with no mathematical knowledge likewise burst into print, expounding pet theories based on personal experience. Lord Rosslyn, for example, claimed to have a system which 'I would be willing to demonstrate in a private room to persons interested in it, who would make it worth my while to do so,' whereby a capital of £15,000 would bring in a return of £1,000 a day. Sir Hiram Maxim questioned this claim. So did many others. 'If Lord Rosslyn is so sure of making money at Monte Carlo, why isn't he down there busy making it?' asked the author of a letter in the correspondence columns of the Paris edition of the *New York Herald*. But even Sir Hiram, who considered all systems 'bad and unprofitable', admitted that a bad one was better than none at all; and this view has been echoed more recently by Charles Graves who contends that at baccara 'it is essential to have some kind of system'.

Almost all the systems in use today are based more or less on the principle of 'doubling up' on an even chance, either after a loss or a win. The following are the best known:

THE MARTINGALE

This system, so called perhaps because it supposedly acts as a curb, either preventing a gambler from 'plunging' or fortune from rearing against him, was known in England as early as 1815, and in *The Newcomes* Thackeray warns against it: 'You have not played as yet? Do not do so; above all avoid a martingale if you do.'

The object is to recoup your losses by doubling your stake after each losing coup until you win, when you start all over again. For example, if you place the minimum of ten francs on one of the *chances simples* and you lose, your next stake will be twenty; if you lose again you then stake forty, and so on. Supposing you win on the fourth coup, when your stake has accordingly increased to eighty francs, you will be paid eighty francs and recover your stake. You will have lost seventy francs on the first three coups, however, so that your net win is actually ten francs, i.e. the amount of your original stake. The result, in fact, is the same as if you had won on the very first coup.

By using the Martingale, therefore, you are theoretically bound to win since the chance on which you have staked is bound to come up in the long run. But the snag is that you have to keep doubling your stake practically, not theoretically; and the consequence, unless you have considerable funds at your disposal, may be alarming. Supposing, for example, you lose nine times running (and a series of this length is not so uncommon as you might think) your total losses will have mounted to 5,110 francs and your stake for the tenth coup will have soared to 5,120 francs – over five hundred times your original unit! – yet this is the amount you must risk in order to win back only ten francs. Moreover, if you lose the tenth coup, your next stake will exceed the maximum allowed by the casino and the system therefore collapses. It collapses even more quickly if your original stake is larger than the minimum allowed, for you then reach the maximum, and thus come to grief, all the sooner.

THE GREAT MARTINGALE

This works on the same principle as the simple Martingale, with the difference that instead of merely doubling your stake after each loss, you double it *and add it to this sum*, thus increasing it at the rate of 1, 3, 7, 15, 31, and so on. Though this enables you to win back a proportionately larger amount than your original unit, you reach the maximum one coup sooner.

THE BOULE DE NEIGE

This is a Martingale in reverse. You leave your stake to double up after each *win*, withdrawing it partially or totally at the end of as many coups as you choose. The greater the profit, the greater the risk; and *vice versa*.

LORD ROSSLYN'S SYSTEM

This is likewise based on a progression. After each coup you increase your stake by one unit – except for the second stake, which must always be three units. If you win this second coup, you will be two units to the good and you then start all over again. If, however, you lose the second coup, your third stake will be four units; if you lose the third coup, your fourth stake will be five units, and so on – except the final stake which you calculate in such a way as to wipe out all previous losses and leave the result of plus one. You will then have gained one unit for every coup played.

For example, your score might be as follows:

First loss . .		-1	and lose. Add 1 more.
		1	
	Total	-2	

Second stake .		-3	and lose.
	Lost	-5	to which add 1 more.
		1	
	Total	-6	

Third stake   .   −4 and lose

              Lost   −10 to which add I more.
                         1

            Total −11

Fourth stake .   +5 and win

              Lost   −6 to which add 1 more.
                         1

            Total   −7

Fifth stake . .   −6 and lose

              Lost   −13 to which add 1 more.
                         1

            Total −14

Sixth stake . .   −7 and lose

              Lost   −21 to which add 1 more.
                         1

            Total −22

Seventh stake .   +8 and win

              Lost   −14 to which add 1 more.
                         1

            Total −15

Eighth stake   .   +9 and win

Lost   −6 to which add 1 more.
          1

Total −7

Ninth stake   .   +8 and win.

Result   +1

Result – Coups won:	4	Units won:	30
Coups lost:	5	Units lost:	21
Total:	9	Gain:	9

(Note that the last stake is only 8 instead of 10. This is because you only require to arrive at a result of plus 1. If you had lost the ninth coup then your stake on the tenth would have been 11, just as if you had staked 10 on the previous coup.)

This system gives you a much longer run for your money than is possible with the Martingale. Since the progression is extremely slow, you can start off with a relatively higher stake, even as much as 1,000 francs (and thus increase your chance of a proportionately larger gain) without reaching the maximum too quickly. But apart from a large capital, it also requires, in Lord Rosslyn's own words, 'perseverance, strong nerves and the constitution of a dray horse'.

THE LABOUCHÈRE OR 'LABBY'

This system was named after Henry Dupré Labouchère, the Victorian journalist and politician, who either invented it or used it regularly. It works on the principle of dividing your stake into three unequal parts, so that although the bank may win more often than you the net result will be in your favour. Any sum may be taken as the basic unit. For the sake of convenience, since ten francs is the minimum allowed, let us call this sum 60 and divide it into 10, 20 and 30.

You write these numbers down on a score sheet and you stake the sum of the two outside ones, i.e. 40 (10 plus 30). If you win, you cross off these two numbers and stake the remaining one, i.e. 20. If you win again, you will have been paid an amount equal to your basic unit of 60, and you start again with 10, 20, 30. On the other hand, if you lose the first coup, you add the amount of your stake, i.e. 40, to your row of figures (which thus becomes 10, 20, 30, 40) and again stake the sum of the outside ones, i.e. 50 (10 plus 40). If you lose again you repeat the process. If you win you again cross off the outside numbers, and so on, until you have gained your basic unit of 60.

This system is far safer than the Martingale. It is also far more tedious and laborious.

FLAT STAKES

Like the Martingale, this system aims at recouping your losses by increasing your stake until you win; but instead of doubling up after each losing coup, you increase your stake only by the amount of your basic unit, and only after losing five coups. You stake one unit at a time, marking down every loss and crossing it out when you win. After, say, four losses and one win, your score sheet would thus read:

1 1 1 1

Supposing you then have two more losses, it would read:

1 1 1 1 1 1

At this stage, since you now have five losses marked down, your next stake will be two units. Supposing you lose twice, you mark down two each time, so that your score sheet will then read:

1 1 1 1 1 1 2 2

Supposing you then win five times in succession, you cross off two after each coup and continue to stake two units at each coup until all the numbers are crossed out, when you will have made a profit of one unit. You then return to staking one at a time. On the other hand, supposing you lose three more times, you mark down three more twos and your score sheet will then read:

1 1 1 1 1 1 2 2 2 2 2

At this stage, since you now have five twos marked down, your next stake will be three units. After each losing coup, you mark down three. After every win you cross off three (three ones, or a two and a one, but never a three until the twos and ones are exhausted) and continue to stake three units at each coup until all the numbers are crossed out when, again, you will have made a profit of one unit.

The advantage of this system is that you are unlikely ever to reach the maximum if you use the minimum stake as your basic unit. On the other hand it is difficult to recoup a long series of losses unless you play for higher stakes and thus abandon the system.

THE D'ALEMBERT OR MONTANT D'ALEMBERT

Named after Jean de Rond d'Alembert, the eighteenth-century French mathematician, this system consists simply of increasing your stake by one unit after every loss and decreasing it by one unit after every win. When you have decreased back to zero, you will have won half a unit for every coup played. Thus, with ten francs as your basic unit, supposing you lose three times in succession and increase by one unit each time, your total loss will be 60 francs (10 plus 20 plus 30) and your next stake will be 40 francs. If you then win four times in succession and decrease by one unit each time, your total win will be 100 francs (40 plus 30 plus 20 plus 10) and on the eighth coup you will have made 40 francs (100 minus 60), i.e. five francs or half your unit for every coup played.

THE PAROLI

This system was known in the eighteenth century in connection with the game of faro or pharaoh (said to be called from the king of hearts being so named) and is mentioned in the letters of Horace Walpole, who was an inveterate player: 'My friendship goes to sleep like a paroli at Pharaoh, and does not wake again until the deal is over.'

Supposing you stake one unit of ten francs and win, your next stake will be your original unit plus your winnings, i.e. twenty francs. Supposing you then win again, you withdraw thirty francs of the forty you have won and start again with your original stake of ten francs. On the other hand, if you lose on the first or second coup, you continue to stake one unit until you have two successive wins – but after losing three times in succession, you start staking two units, and so on, until you have two successive wins – when you again withdraw all but ten francs of your winnings and start again with your original stake, making a profit of twenty francs each time.

This system is preferred by many big gamblers.

TIERS ET TOUT À LA BOULE DE NEIGE
Like the 'Labby', this system consists of dividing your stake – but only in two parts, of one-third and two-thirds respectively. For example, supposing you first stake ten francs and lose, your next stake will be twenty francs. Whether you win or lose on this second coup, you then revert to your original unit of ten francs. If you lose, you at least limit your loss for the series to thirty francs, and if you win, you make a profit of ten francs. On the other hand, supposing you win on the first coup, your next stake will again be twenty francs, i.e. your original unit and your winnings. Again, whether you win or lose on this second coup, you then revert to your original unit of ten francs. If you lose, your total loss for the series is no more than your original stake of ten francs; and if you win, you make a profit of thirty francs.

This system was used successfully by García at Homburg and, occasionally, by Wells at Monte Carlo.

REVERSE SYSTEMS
All these systems can be played in reverse, i.e. you can *decrease* your stake after a loss and increase it after a *win*. This method –

first advocated by the Hon S. R. Beresford in 1926 – is psychologically advantageous; by reversing a system, you in effect compel the bank to play it against you, instead of the other way about. You make no attempt to chase your losses but set out to exploit your wins, and instead of trying to rake in small sums steadily (but with the risk of striking a fatal losing run) you resign yourself to losing a small sum daily (but with the chance of striking a favourable sequence which will allow you either to break the table or reach the maximum).

But in practice, even if you play for twelve hours a day, you may not strike a winning run soon enough to make up for the dreary succession of small losses you will have meanwhile sustained.

There are many other systems, cryptically or alluringly named, such as The Breadwinner, The Chaser and vb's, but they are not worth describing in detail since each of them is a variation of one or another of those listed above. As can be seen, they are all supposedly based on the Law of Probabilities. This law is an accurate statement of certain mathematical truths, but is misinterpreted by most players because they are unaware of the technicalities of gambling and ignorant even of the usual terms employed. These are as follows:

L'équilibre is the constant equilibrium subsisting between a pair of *chances simples*, i.e. *rouge* and *noir*, *pair* and *impair*, or *passe* and *manque*. This equilibrium is occasionally disturbed by one or the other of a pair occurring with undue frequency, but in the end it is always re-established. For example, *rouge* may occur several times running; but, however long this run, it will in the end be balanced by a similar run of *noir*. The same applies to the *chances multiples*, i.e. *colonnes*, *douzaines*, *sixains*, *transversales* and single numbers.

La vibration is the term used to express the arbitrary and incalculable order in the occurrence of *chances simples*. For example, *rouge* may occur three times running, then *noir* once, then *rouge* again three times, then *noir* six times. Similarly, though the probability in each coup of any particular number occurring is thirty-six to one, 22 has been recorded six times in succession and zero has been known to occur three times in five successive coups.

L'écart refers to the deviation from the Law of Probabilities which is constantly tending towards the establishment of the *équilibre*. The action of this law would in theory secure that *rouge* and *noir* should each occur alternately fifty times in one hundred coups. In fact this hardly ever happens. For example, if in a hundred coups *rouge* occurs 42 times, and *noir* 58, the *écart* is said to be 16 against *rouge* and in favour of *noir*.

L'oscillation is the movement resulting from the everlasting conflict between the *écart* and the *équilibre*. For example, if *rouge* occurs six times running, then *noir* once, then *rouge* again six times, then *noir* twice, i.e. twelve *rouge* and three *noir*, there is an *oscillation* resulting in an *écart* of nine against *noir*. Supposing this run is immediately followed by one *rouge*, then five successive *noir*, then one *rouge* and six successive *noir*, i.e. two *rouge* and eleven *noir*, there is an *oscillation* in the contrary direction which momentarily re-establishes the *équilibre*.

La série is the number of times in succession that one or the other of a pair of *chances simples* occurs. For example, three *noir* occurring one after the other form a *série*, or run, of three black; five consecutive *rouge* make a red *série* of five.

L'intermittence refers to the temporary alternation of a pair of *chances simples*, for example one *rouge*, followed by one *noir*, followed by one *rouge*, and so on. Similarly, if for a time the chances occur twice in regular alternation, e.g. two *rouge*, followed by two *noir*, and so on, this is known as an *intermittence de deux*.

La marche is the decision as to where the stake is to be laid, e.g. on *rouge* or on *noir*. *La gagnante* is the method of always staking on the colour which has just occurred, *la perdante* on the colour that has just lost, *l'avant-dernier* on the colour which occurred the last coup but one.

La progression or *le massage* refers to the number of units, i.e. the exact sum of money, to be staked at each coup.

As can be seen, each of the factors listed above plays a significant part in any system. The *écart*, for example, frequently reaches large proportions and, although it is in theory eventually annulled by a temporary re-establishment of the *équilibre*, this may not happen until it can be of no practical use to the gambler. Similarly, though every system is based on the probability of the continuance of a *série* or *intermittence*, a gambler banking on a long series comes to grief when the game becomes persistently intermittent, and *vice versa*.

Every system is also based upon the combination of the *marche* and the *progression*, since considering the advantage to the bank derived from the *refait* and the zero and the maximum – factors which likewise have to be taken into account – there is no possibility of winning by consistently staking the same sum. Yet as can be seen from the description of the eight basic systems listed in the previous section, the progression of the Martingale, for example, and still more so that of the Great Martingale, is dangerously rapid; while the d'Alembert, though comprising a far slower progression, is particularly affected by the *écart*.

Yet another factor which affects all systems is the vast advantage accruing to the bank from its command of a capital infinitely greater than that of the average or even the richest gambler. Anyone with limited funds may quail at the prospect of staking more than five thousand francs in order to recover a basic unit of only ten francs – knowing, moreover, that if he loses again, his next stake is bound to exceed the maximum – yet this situation has been known to confront many a player using the Martingale. Furthermore, any sum of money has a relatively different value depending on whether it is won or lost. For example, if you start with a capital of one hundred francs and win fifty, you will have increased your funds by one third; but if instead of winning, you lose the same sum, you will have decreased the same capital by one half. This difference may have an important psychological effect on any gambler.

The bank derives an additional psychological superiority from its machine-like impassivity as opposed to the human emotions to which the individual player is necessarily a prey. The latter, admittedly, has the advantage of being able to decide for himself how much money he will risk, on which chance he will stake, at which hour of the day he will start to play, and for how long he will continue, none of which choices are open to the bank; but this advantage is in the end nullified by what Victor Silberer calls the regular, passionless process of the lifeless machine.

Though the Law of Probabilities is frequently misunderstood or misinterpreted, there can be no ambiguity in calculating the probable frequency of a series of even chances. In fact it is a very simple matter. Supposing play is about to begin at roulette or trente-et-quarante, the chance that *rouge* will occur on the first coup is equal to the chance of *noir* occurring. In other words, the probability of either colour occurring is 1:2. For the second coup, the calculation is equally simple. The probability of the same colour appearing a second time is $\frac{1}{2} \times \frac{1}{2}$, in other words 1:4. Similarly, the probability of a series of three is 1:8, of a series of four 1:16, and so on. From this the following table may be constructed:

Series	Probability	Series	Probability
1	1:2	11	1:2,048
2	1:4	12	1:4,096
3	1:8	13	1:8,192
4	1:16	14	1:16,384
5	1:32	15	1:32,768
6	1:64	16	1:65,536
7	1:128	17	1:131,072
8	1:256	18	1:262,144
9	1:512	19	1:524,288
10	1:1,024	20	1:1,048,576

(For the sake of convenience, this table does not take into account zero or the *refait*, which in fact considerably increases the probability against a long series.)

This table shows that the longer the series the more seldom it occurs, and this is also confirmed by statistics. A player, having witnessed a series of nine *rouge*, may therefore argue that *noir* is more likely to occur at the next coup, since *rouge* has only one chance in over a thousand of occurring a tenth time. This argument is based on what some gamblers call 'the maturity of the chances'. At first sight it seems logical, proved by calculation and borne out by statistical evidence. Yet it is radically and dangerously false.

A moment's reflection will show that no coup can be affected by a previous coup or series of coups; that every coup is in fact an isolated chance, uninfluenced by and independent of the coups that have preceded it; and that therefore after a series of nine *rouge* – or, for that matter, after a series of nineteen or ninety – the probability of *noir* occurring at the next coup is in reality nothing more than an even chance. For, in the case of roulette, for example, however long the series of *rouge* may have been, it will in no way have altered the size or shape or consistency of the wheel. The red compartments will be exactly as they were before, they will still number precisely eighteen, they will still alternate perfectly with the black compartments. It follows, therefore, that at the next spin the ball, which likewise will not have been altered in any way by the length of the series, will stand just as good a chance of dropping into a red compartment as it did before. And the same applies in the case of trente-et-quarante. The six packs of cards will not have been altered in any way by the length of the series. Their number will be exactly the same as before. The colour and value of each card will be the same as before. The cards will remain in the order in which they were shuffled, and those remaining will in no way be affected by the ones that have already been dealt. It follows, therefore, that at the next deal the bottom row will stand just as good a chance of coming out closest to thirty-one as it did before.

The misconception of most players in this respect consists in their deducing, from the rareness of a long series, the conclusion that the probability of a series ending increases with every successive coup that prolongs it. This is not so. In fact, the improbability of a series continuing decreases with each successive coup that prolongs it.

For example, experience and theory agree in showing that a series of ten *rouge* will occur on an average only once in 1,024 times. But the probability against a series of ten, which was indeed 1,024:1 before it had begun, has been successively reduced in the last nine coups to an even chance of 1:1. The result of the coup which, with the occurrence of *rouge*, started the series was to reduce the probability from 1,024:1 to 512:1; for, *rouge* having already occurred once, only nine repetitions were needed to complete the number. After the second occurrence of *rouge*, the probability against a series of ten fell to 256:1, and, similarly, after the third occurrence, to 128:1, after the fourth, to 64:1; after the fifth, to 32:1; after the sixth, to 16:1; after the seventh, to 8:1; after the ninth, to 2:1; and after the tenth, to 1:1, in other words the chances became even.

From this it can be seen that the theoretical probability against a series of any given length exists *only before that series has begun*. After *rouge* has occurred any number of times in succession, the chance that it will occur again at the next coup is always an even chance, i.e. 1:1.

While admitting that this may be mathematically true, the apostles of the 'evening up' theory and those who believe in 'the maturity of the chances' contend that in practice the longer a series is the more seldom it occurs. In fact, according to the *permanences* (the records of the bank which are published every week) an even chance has never been known to occur more than twenty-eight consecutive times. *But this*, as Victor Silberer is careful to point out, *does not imply that a longer series never can or never will occur.*

The apostles of the 'evening up' theory also contend that however many times *rouge* may occur, in succession or otherwise, *noir* will in the end occur an equal number of times; or, as Lord Rosslyn put it: 'If you toss a coin into the air a thousand times, it will come down head five hundred times and tail five hundred times.' And so it may. On the other hand, it may just as well come down seven hundred times head and only three hundred times tail, though in practice such a deviation – 20 per cent – would be rare. Indeed, from a study of the *permanences* in the summer of 1892, the mathematician Karl Pearson discovered that in 16,019 spins of the roulette wheel, *rouge* occurred 8,053 times – a deviation of only 0.27 per cent. A similar study of the *permanences* during various other periods of that year yielded much the same result, from which Professor Pearson concluded that in respect of the average total numbers of *rouge* and *noir*, roulette did in fact obey the theoretical Law of Probabilities, that is to say that the *équilibre* did exist. At the same time, however, he discovered that series of four and under occurred less frequently, series of between five and eleven far less frequently, and intermittences far more frequently, in practice than in theory – the deviation from the theoretical norm in the latter case being so great as to 'set the laws of chance at defiance in the most persistent and remarkable manner.' In fact, in respect of one particular fortnight's play, the professor declared: 'If Monte Carlo roulette had gone on since the beginning of geological time on earth, we should not have expected such an occurrence to have occurred *once* on the supposition that the game is one of chance.'

A fortnight, however, is only a small fraction of time arbitrarily marked off in the infinite stream of ever-continuing play and, within the limits of such short periods, occurrences which contradict the Law of Probabilities are only to be expected. Calculations based on this law are to be relied upon for *approximate* accuracy only when long periods of play are considered, for *absolute* accuracy only when the period considered is infinite. Given the relatively short span of human life, it is therefore impossible for any player to be accurate in his calculations. For, as Sir Hiram Maxim aptly asks, how can a player know that the evening-up will take place at the same table? 'Why not on some other table at some other time? Then, again, when there is an abnormal run of any chance, how is he to know that this run is not in itself an act of evening-up to balance a run that took place last year at Ostend, or perhaps in far-away China twenty years ago?' He may be convinced that he is operating in accordance with a scientific application of an incontrovertible mathematical law; but this conviction, according to Herr Silberer, is based on a faulty premise. Even with the systematic method, a player's success or failure depends on his luck rather than his skill; for it depends on the tendency of the *écart* during the period of his operations. He will be successful only if this is favourable to him, in other words only if he happens to be what gamblers call 'in the vein'.

Certain players seem to be consistently 'in the vein'. Their luck seems to be such that they always win even when the chances against them are a million to one. Supposing, for instance, that twenty million people engage in a game of Pitch and Toss, playing against one another two at a time; supposing that these same twenty million continue to play against one another, the pairs of contestants being different at each toss of the coin; and supposing that there are twenty such contests and only about twenty out of the twenty million players win all twenty times – then surely those winners will be accounted exceptionally lucky. For not only is each of them literally one in a million, but also, as can be seen from the table on p. 181, a series of twenty will occur on an average only once in over a million times.

Yet it can be argued that in such a case so-called luck has no bearing on the result, which, according to the Law of Probabilities, is *bound* to be what it is; i.e. about twenty out of the twenty million players are *bound* to win twenty times in succession, *for the very reason that* a series of twenty will occur on an average about once in a million times. Moreover this can be demonstrated by the following logical process:

After the first contest there will be ten million winners and ten million losers. After the second the result will be the same, i.e. exactly half of the players will win. And of these ten million winners of the second contest, approximately one half, i.e. about five million, will also have won the first. Similarly, after the third contest about two and a half million will have won all three, and so on, until, after the twentieth contest about twenty players will be found to have won all twenty times.

As can be seen, this result is inevitable, dictated by mathematics and in no way dependent on individual luck. To reason otherwise is a fallacy. But there are people who always have, and still do, reason otherwise and who would surely account twenty winners out of twenty million players exceptionally lucky – not only in the sense of being lucky because they *have* won, but of being *likelier to win* at any time than any of the other twenty million, i.e. that they are *naturally* luckier than the latter. Yet the success of the twenty shows only that they *have been* lucky, not that they *are* lucky by nature nor that they are likely to be lucky again.

To look upon luck as some sort of mysterious personal attribute is therefore sheer superstition. But then gamblers are notoriously superstitious. A miniature equestrian statue of Louis xiv, in bronze, was placed in the lobby of the Hôtel de Paris in Monte Carlo in 1907. Since then the horse's bent knee has been rubbed so often 'for luck' that it now shines like gold.

Even players who would never admit to being superstitious sometimes have some specially lucky number or numbers of their own and make a point of following it. Bill Darnborough, said to have been 'probably the most remarkable gambler that ever went into the casino at Monte Carlo', invariably backed several numbers at a time, but only those of the last dozen. Arthur de Rothschild always staked on 17. There are other players who, though not favouring any special number, have a particular foible or prejudice in which they indulge. The Grand Duke Nicholas of Russia always staked in the same manner, covering any single number in every possible way; first the number itself, then *à cheval*, then on the *carré*, the *transversale*, and so on. Cornelius Vanderbilt likewise always staked on a *transversale* and, like the grand duke, never sat down to gamble but moved away from the table after placing his money. The Grand Duke Michael, on the other hand, always sat down, but only at the end of the table; while his mother made a point of sitting near the middle and never placed her own stakes but handed her money to one of the croupiers to stake for her.

At one time, it is said, the clergyman of the English church at Monte Carlo never gave out any hymns under number 36, for fear that some of his congregation might note down the numbers with a view to backing them at roulette. And even today many a player can be found who will stake on a particular number because it confronts him in a curiously persistent way. He may back 18, for example, simply because the number of his sleeping-berth on the train to Monte Carlo was 18 and he was put into room No. 18

at the Hôtel de Paris on the day of his arrival, the 18th of the month. This is no worse a method of staking than many so-called systems.

As can be seen, then, there are three main schools of thought concerning gambling: the scientists, like Victor Silberer and Karl Pearson, who contend that games of chance are governed by well-defined (but often misinterpreted) mathematical laws; the school of thought represented by Lord Rosslyn and his successors, who believe that a system can be found which, if not infallible, is consistently successful; and finally those who believe that every spin of the wheel, every deal of the cards, is regulated by pure and simple luck. Against these three conflicting views there is the undeniable fact that there have been, and still are, a few players – the *licenciés ès roulette* – who consistently make a modest living from the tables. But even their achievement, according to Sir Hiram Maxim, can be partially explained by the Law of Probabilities.

Supposing, for example, that 1,024 players, each with a capital of 10,240 francs, set themselves the target of winning forty francs each per day for their living expenses by playing the Martingale with ten francs as their basic unit. Now it has been shown that a capital of 10,240 francs would be exhausted by an adverse series of ten coups; and according to the table on p. 181 the probability of a series of ten occurring is 1:1,024. It is therefore probable that one of the 1,024 players will lose his capital on the first day. After 512 days, 512 players will probably have lost their capital. And after each successive period of 512 days, half of the remainder will probably have lost theirs. Thus after 1,024 days, 256 more players will have lost their capital; after 1,536 days, 128 more, and so on – until after 5,120 days all but one will have lost their capital.

For the sake of convenience this calculation does not take into consideration the *refait*, which in practice would reduce the 5,120 days to 4,403, or, say, twelve years. Under these conditions, however, there would be an even chance that one of the 1,024 players would survive twelve years. On this basis there would be one chance in four that he would survive twenty-four years, one in eight that he would survive forty-eight years, one chance in sixteen that he would survive ninety-six years – which, as Sir Hiram concludes, 'is no more of a miracle than a series of five which occurs several times every day'.

Whether it is true or not that a bad system is better than none, it is undeniable that some methods of staking are better than others. Since the bank has an advantage over you at every coup, the fewer coups you play the more chance you have of winning. Your chance of winning is also in proportion to the amount by which you wish to increase your original stake. If you play only to double it, and stake only once, you stand an almost even chance of doing so. On the other hand, if you 'plaster the board', i.e. place small sums on several numbers at a time, in the hope that one of them turns up, you increase the bank's advantage proportionately and therefore decrease your own chances of winning.

Yet Bill Darnborough always staked in this manner.

Never before or since have such masses of gold and notes been heaped upon a roulette table. The most astonishing feature of his operations was the lightning speed with which he placed his stakes. He would start as soon as the croupier began to spin, continuing to dab the board with piles of money until the *rien ne va plus* was enforced.

But his success year after year – he is said to have won over two million francs during a lifetime spent at the tables – only proves that he was an exception to the rule. His luck was legendary. One summer day in 1909 he noticed a friend's sports car drawn up outside the Hôtel de Paris and offered to buy it for twelve thousand francs – 'if you will wait,' he added, 'while I pop over to the bank,' by which he meant the casino. He made the sum at one coup by staking the maximum at trente-et-quarante: the only time he had ever played that game.

Considering the construction of the roulette wheel and the manner in which the game is played, no croupier can possibly spin the ball so as to cause it to fall into any particular side of the wheel, still less select a single number or small group of numbers.

Yet many players believe that croupiers, from sheer mechanical habit, may unwittingly do so. Some therefore play *voisins*, that is they stake on the number that last came up and on one or more of the four numbers on each side of it on the wheel; while others stake on 'distances' or even on 'opposites' from the last number. Some, again, stake on *les numéros dominantes*, i.e. the numbers that occur most frequently; others on *les numéros en retard*, i.e. those that have not yet occurred. Yet another way of staking is on *les finales* – *les finales dominantes* or *les finales en retard*. For example, if 7 occurs you then stake on *les finales sept*, i.e. 7, 17 and 27. But these manners of staking are derived more from superstition than from method, and are no less unreasonable than 'plastering the board'.

Any method, in fact, which involves staking on two or more chances at a time is wrong in principle. Yet many players make a habit of staking, for example, on *rouge* and *impair* simultaneously in the belief that this is a particularly safe method on account of what they call its 'stability'. If a number comes up that is red and uneven, they double both stakes; if it is black and even, they lose both; if it is red and even, or black and uneven, they neither win nor lose since in both cases the winning of the one chance is set off against the loss of the other. It is the relatively large proportion of these *coups neutres* that is responsible for the popular misconception as to the safety of this method.

But a moment's reflection will show that all these *coups neutres*, which at first sight seem to cost nothing, do on the contrary increase the cost since in effect they double the advantage of the bank. For at each coup there are four possible results – *rouge* and *impair*, *noir* and *impair*, *rouge* and *pair*, and *noir* and *pair* – of which one will yield a profit, one a loss, and two will be neutral. At each coup, therefore, one half of the total amount staked is employed for an entirely profitless operation, but is none the less exposed to the risk of the zero.

Similarly, though many players also make a habit of staking *à cheval* on the columns or on the dozens, for the satisfaction of winning more often than they lose, this method is even worse than staking on two or more even chances. For, although they will win on an average two coups for every one they lose, the profit is only half the amount of the stake, while their loss on the occurrence of the zero is enormous in proportion to the amount they stand to win.

Yet there is a method whereby you can obtain the same result in the case of a win and yet avoid the total loss caused by the zero. For example, instead of placing your full stake *à cheval* on the two first dozens, you ought to place three quarters of it on *manque* and the remaining quarter on the *sixain* 19 to 24. Supposing your stake is four units, if you place all four *à cheval* on the first two dozens and you win, you will be paid two units more. So you will then have six units. Supposing, on the other hand, you place three units on *manque* and one unit on the *sixain* 19 to 24, if you win on *manque* you will be paid three units more and will then have six units; and if you win on the *sixain* you will be paid five units more and will likewise have six units – i.e. exactly the same sum as if you had played on the two dozens *à cheval*. Similarly, instead of placing your full stake *à cheval* on the two last dozens, you ought to place three quarters of it on *passe* and one quarter on the *sixain* 13 to 18. Again, if you win in either case you will be paid exactly the same as if you had played on the two dozens *à cheval*.

But supposing zero occurs. If you have placed all four units on two dozens *à cheval* you will lose all four, since all stakes except *chances simples* are then swept off the board. But if you have divided your stake between *manque* and the corresponding *sixain* (or on *passe* and the corresponding *sixain*) you will lose the one unit staked on the *sixain* and only half of the three on *manque* or on *passe*. Thus you will have saved one and a half of your four units, i.e. $37\frac{1}{2}$ per cent of your total stake.

This is a striking example of a method being, in theory and in practice, *infallibly* better than another. For it minimizes the effects of the bank's advantage, and this is the most that anyone can hope to do.

Finally, an alternative to staking individually against the bank is to join forces with other gamblers and play in syndicate. Though syndicates have come to grief at the tables with as much regularity as individual gamblers, there are many arguments in favour of pooling resources. Apart from the larger capital provided by a syndicate, the feeling of solidarity engendered by concerted action is a psychological advantage. Also the mental and physical strain of systematic play is lessened by being shared among others: two people playing in consecutive shifts of six hours each are less prone to fatigue than one person playing for twelve hours at a stretch. But, most importantly, any syndicate of six members or more is able to back all six *chances simples* simultaneously, thereby increasing the likelihood of winning on at least one of them. This was recently suggested in theory, and later confirmed in practice, by an English syndicate headed by a certain Norman Leigh.

Leigh had worked out that a single individual backing one *chance simple* for twelve hours a day would lose on an average for five days before striking a winning run. From this he concluded that one of six players, backing all six *chances simples* simultaneously, was bound to strike a winning run at least once daily. He chose and trained a team of twelve, so as to cover all six *chances simples* in two shifts of six hours each, and proceeded to apply his method at the Casino Municipal in Nice.

Starting with a capital of 1,200 francs each, playing the Reverse Labouchère and staking an initial unit of five francs, his syndicate won more than eight hundred thousand in eight days. They were then banned from the gaming rooms by the management. Whether they would have gone on winning, no one can tell. The action taken against them shows that the casino feared they might. It also shows that no matter how successful a system may be the bank will always have the last word.

BIBLIOGRAPHY
AND REFERENCES

CHAPTER ONE

For information on the House of Grimaldi I have drawn on the court historian Henri Métivier: *Monaco et ses princes*, 2 vols, 1865; and also, as a counterbalance to this official and often sycophantic history, on Abel Rendu: *Menton et Monaco*, 1867. Later authorities include Gustave Saige: *Monaco, ses origines et son histoire*, 1897; and Léon-Honoré Labande: *Histoire de la principauté de Monaco*, 1924. The first ten chapters of Adolphe Smith, *Monaco and Monte Carlo*, 1912, also deal with the history of Monaco.

Page 9: Florestan quoted in Dr Poumiès de la Siboutie, *Souvenirs d'un médecin de Paris*, 1910, p. 360.

Page 10: *Rabagas* by Victorien Sardou, first performed at the Vaudeville Theatre, Paris, on 1 February 1872.

CHAPTER TWO

For descriptions of mid-nineteenth century Monaco, see Théodore de Banville: *La Mer de Nice*, 1860; and Marie de Saint-Germain: *Monaco 1860–1875*, 1875.

Page 17: Smollett: *Travels in France and Italy*, 1766, OUP, 1907, p. 193.

Page 17: 'Newborough'. See Charles Graves: *Royal Riviera*, Heinemann, 1957, p. 36.

Pages 18–23: For information on the early days of the Monaco casino I have drawn almost exclusively on Count Egon Corti: *The*

Wizard of Homburg and Monte Carlo, Thornton and Butterworth, 1935, the only detailed work on the subject. All quotations are from this, unless otherwise stated. For additional material see Charles Limousin: *Almanach illustré de Monaco et Monte Carlo*, 1895; *Guide du Joueur*, 1899; and *De Monte Carlo à Beausoleil*, 1908; also Adolphe Smith, op. cit.

Page 23: This quotation from the court historian is typical of Métivier's repeated attempts to run with the hare and hunt with the hounds by condemning gambling and at the same time condoning the Prince of Monaco's grant of a gaming concession.

CHAPTER THREE

Page 24: Quotation from Charles Graves: *The Big Gamble*, Hutchinson, 1951, p. 41.

Page 24: Madame de Sévigné: *Lettres*, 3 vols, 1925, vol. iii. p. 94.

Page 24: Madame de Genlis: *Adèle et Théodore ou Lettres sur l'education*, 2 vols, 1782, vol. ii, pp. 217–18.

CHAPTER FOUR

Unless otherwise stated, all information on François Blanc is drawn from Corti, op. cit. For additional material, see Charles Kingston: *The Romance of Monte Carlo*, Bodley Head, 1925.

Pages 38–42: For information on gambling in general, see Andrew Steinmetz: *The Gaming Table*, 2 vols, Tinsley, 1870; and Ralph Nevill: *Light Come, Light Go*, Macmillan, 1909.

Page 38: Henri IV. See Hardouin de Péréfixe: *Histoire ed Henri le Grand*, 1812.

Page 40: *L'encyclopédie ou dictionnaire raisonné des sciences, des arts et des métiers, par une société des gens de lettres. Mis en ordre par M. Diderot, et, quant à la partie mathématique, par M. d'Alembert, 35 vols*, 1751–80.

Page 48: Charles Graves: *The Big Gamble*, p. 54.

Page 49: The contemporary eye-witness was George Augustus Sala: *Make Your Game*, Ward and Lock, 1860, p. 186.

Page 50: Dostoevsky: *The Gambler*, 1862, tr. by Constance Garnett, Heinemann, 1917, p. 63.

Pages 50–2: For information on García, see Corti: op. cit. and Adrien Mercier du Pis, *Du Jeu*, 1881.

Page 52: Contemporary observer quoted by Richard Proctor: *Chance and Luck*, Longmans, 1887.

CHAPTER FIVE

Page 56: Blanc's offer. St-Germain: op. cit., p. 35.

Page 56: Press report. *Journal de Monaco*, 5 April 1863.

CHAPTER SIX

Page 61: Lord Brougham: *The Nineteenth Century*, Feb. 1890.

Page 61: Sir Charles Dilke: *The Fall of Prince Florestan of Monaco*, 1874, p. 25.

Page 61: Blanc's spectacles described in Carlo de Perrières: *Rien ne va plus*, 1875, p. 46; Blanc's gait in Limousin: *Almanach*, p. 56.

Pages 62–3: Dostoevsky: *Letters to his Family and Friends*, tr. by E. C. Mayne, 1914; *Letters to his Wife*, tr. by E. Hill and D. Mudie, 1930.

Page 64: *Franglais. Journal de Monaco*, 7 June 1868.

Page 70: Closing of kursaal. Nevill, op. cit., p. 308.

CHAPTER SEVEN

Page 73: Saxon-les-Bains. W. T. A. Stamer: *A Day at Monte Carlo*, 1894, p. 65.

Page 73: Condamine building lots. Stamer: op. cit., p. 35.

Page 74: Pastoral letter. *The Times*, 11 March 1876.

Page 75: Article in *The Guardian*, 26 April 1876.

Pages 75–7: For information on Jaggers, see Graves: *Big Gamble*, pp. 76–7; Kingston, op. cit., pp. 197–200; and General Pierre Polovtsoff: *Monte Carlo Casino*, Stanley Paul, 1937, pp. 173–5.

CHAPTER EIGHT

Pages 80–2: Construction of the theatre described in Smith: op. cit., pp. 315–20.

Page 81: Marie Blanc's remark reported in Graves: *Big Gamble*, p. 81.

Page 82: Ecstatic outburst: Stamer: op. cit., p. 16.

Page 82: Osbert Sitwell: *The Scarlet Tree*, Macmillan, 1946, p. 234.

Page 85: Queen Victoria's visit reported in *The Evening News*, 12 February 1883.

Page 88: Fatal casualties mentioned in Graves: *Royal Riviera*, p. 117. For further details of the earthquake, see, among others, Polovtsoff: op. cit., pp. 45–6.

Page 89: For a fuller description of Princess Alice, see George W. Herald and Edward D. Rabin: *The Big Wheel*, Morrow, New York, 1963, pp. 45–65.

CHAPTER NINE

Pages 93–6: For Wells's exploit, see Charles Graves: *Big Gamble*; Kingston: op. cit.; Polovtsoff: op. cit.; Nevill: op. cit., etc. Physical description in James Peddie: *All About Monte Carlo – The Extraordinary Career of Charles Wells*, Comet Publishing Company, 1893.

Page 97: German excursionists. Nevill: op. cit., p. 333.

Page 98: Sir Hiram Maxim: *Monte Carlo Facts and Fallacies*, Grant Richards, 1904, pp. 231–2.

Page 99: All-Red Dinner described in J. Rey: *The Whole Art of Dining*, Carmona and Baker, 1914, pp. 133–4.

Pages 100–2: Swindle described in Kingston: op. cit., pp. 201–4.

Page 102: Prince Albert of Monaco: *La Carrière d'un navigateur*, 1902, p. 92.

Page 105: Art of spinning the wheel described in Graves: *Big Gamble*, p. 113.

CHAPTER TEN

Page 107: Young English debutante. Dorothy Peel: *Life's Enchanted Cup*, John Lane, 1933, p. 121.

Page 108: Menu listed in Graves: *Big Gamble*, p. 110.

Page 109: Duchess of Marlborough. Consuelo Vanderbilt Balsan: *The Glitter and the Gold*, Heinemann, 1953, p. 48.

Page 110: La Belle Otero. See Caroline Otero: *My Story*,

Philpot, 1927, pp. 84–5. Anecdote quoted with variations in Herald and Rabin: op. cit., p. 39; and Cornelia Otis Skinner: *Elegant Wits and Grand Horizontals*, Houghton Mifflin, Boston, 1962, p. 236.

Page 111: Monégasque authorities. Kingston: op. cit., p. 83.

Pages 112–13: Goold scandal reported in Kingston: op. cit., Polovtsoff: op. cit., etc.

Pages 115–16: Suicides. See Smith: op. cit., pp. 403–6.

CHAPTER ELEVEN

Page 118: Monte Carlo at the outbreak of the First World War described in Kingston: op. cit., p. 213; and Paul Ketchiva: *The Devil's Playground*, Sampson Low, 1934, p. 12.

Page 119: Mata Hari incident reported in Herald and Rabin: op. cit., pp. 96–102; and Ketchiva: op. cit., p. 154. Further information in Sam Waagenaar: *The Murder of Mata Hari*, Arthur Barker, 1964.

Page 119: For further information on Zaharoff, see Richard Lewisham: *The Man Behind the Scenes*, Gollancz, 1929; Robert Neumann: *Zaharoff, the Armaments King*, tr. by R. T. Clark, Allen and Unwin, 1938; and Donald McCormick: *Pedlar of Death*, Macdonald, 1965.

Page 123: Polovtsoff: op. cit., p. 203.

Pages 124–5: Elsa Maxwell: *I Married the World*, Heinemann, 1955.

Page 125: Country Club described in Graves: *Big Gamble*, p. 145.

Page 128: Clientèle of main casino described in Graves: *Big Gamble*, p. 148.

Page 130: Monte Carlo in Second World War described in Graves: *Big Gamble*, p. 164; and in Herald and Rabin: op. cit., pp. 147–8.

CHAPTER TWELVE

Page 133: American observer. Geoffrey Bocca: *Bikini Beach*, McGraw-Hill, New York, 1962, p. 148.

Page 134: Onassis quoted by J. Bryan III: 'Onassis' in *Holiday*, New York, December 1958. For further information on Onassis, see Goronwy Rees: *The Multi-Millionaires*, Chatto and Windus, 1961, and Willi Frischauer: *Onassis*, Bodley Head, 1968.

Page 135: The only biography of Prince Rainier is by Peter Hawkins: *Prince Rainier of Monaco*, William Kimber, 1966.

Page 138: Livanos. Herald and Rabin: op. cit., p. 229.

Page 140: *Sunday Telegraph*, 2 June 1965.

Page 141: Prince quoted in Hawkins: op. cit., p. 74.

Page 141: Croupier strike reported in *The Times*, 28 May 1966.

Page 142: Onassis quoted by J. Bryan III: op. cit.

CASINO GAMES

For the sections on Roulette and Trente-et-Quarante, I have relied exclusively on Victor Silberer: *The Games of Roulette and Trente-et-Quarante as Played at Monte Carlo*, Harrison, 1910.

For the section on Baccara, I have drawn on Charles Graves: *None but the Rich*, Cassell, 1963.

For the section on Craps, I have referred to Horace C. Levinson: *The Science of Chance*, Faber, 1952.

All quotations are from these three books respectively.

SYSTEMS, CHANCE AND LUCK

Page 169: Dostoevsky: *Gambler*, p. 9.

Page 169: System players described by Herbert Vivian in *The Candid Friend*, 1 February 1902.

Page 170: Lord Rosslyn quoted in Maxim: op. cit., p. 70.

Page 170: Charles Graves: *None but the Rich*, p. 6.

Page 178: S. R. Beresford: *The Future at Monte Carlo*, Palmer, Sutton, 1926.

Pages 178–9: For the section on the Law of Probabilities, I have relied almost entirely on Victor Silberer: op. cit.

Page 183: Karl Pearson: 'Science and Monte Carlo' in *The Fortnightly Review*, February 1894.

Page 185: Game of Pitch and Toss discussed in Richard Proctor: *Chance and Luck*, Longmans, 1887, pp. 5–12.

Page 186: Darnborough. S. R. Beresford: *Beresford's Monte Carlo*, Nice, 1923.

Page 188: Darnborough's method of staking described in S. R. Beresford: op. cit., p. 280.

Page 191: Norman Leigh: *Thirteen Against the Bank*, Weidenfeld and Nicolson, 1976.

INDEX